Comments on other *Amazing Stories* from readers & reviewers

"Tightly written volumes filled with lots of wit and humour about famous and infamous Canadians."
Eric Shackleton, *The Globe and Mail*

"The heightened sense of drama and intrigue, combined with a good dose of human interest is what sets Amazing Stories *apart."*
Pamela Klaffke, *Calgary Herald*

"This is popular history as it should be... For this price, buy two and give one to a friend."
Terry Cook, a reader from Ottawa, on **Rebel Women**

"Glasner creates the moment of the explosion itself in graphic detail...she builds detail upon gruesome detail to create a convincingly authentic picture."
Peggy McKinnon, *The Sunday Herald*, on **The Halifax Explosion**

"It was wonderful...I found I could not put it down. I was sorry when it was completed."
Dorothy F. from Manitoba on **Marie-Anne Lagimodière**

"Stories are rich in description, and bristle with a clever, stylish realness."
Mark Weber, *Central Alberta Advisor*, on **Ghost Town Stories II**

"A compelling read. Bertin...has selected only the most intriguing tales, which she narrates with a wealth of detail."
Joyce Glasner, *New Brunswick Reader*, on **Strange Events**

"The resulting book is one readers will want to share with all the women in their lives."
Lynn Martel, *Rocky Mountain Outlook*, on **Women Explorers**

STOLEN HORSES

STOLEN HORSES

Intiguing Tales of Rustling
and Rescues

ANIMAL/CRIME

by Dorothy Pedersen

PUBLISHED BY ALTITUDE PUBLISHING CANADA LTD.
1500 Railway Avenue, Canmore, Alberta T1W 1P6
www.altitudepublishing.com
1-800-957-6888

Extreme care has been taken to ensure that all information presented in
this book is accurate and up to date. Neither the author nor the
publisher can be held responsible for any errors.

Publisher	Stephen Hutchings
Associate Publisher	Kara Turner
Series Editor	Jill Foran

We acknowledge the financial support of the Government
of Canada through the Book Publishing Industry Development
Program (BPIDP) for our publishing activities.

Altitude GreenTree Program
Altitude Publishing will plant twice as many trees as were used
in the manufacturing of this product.

National Library of Canada Cataloguing in Publication Data

Pedersen, Dorothy
Stolen horses / Dorothy Pedersen.

(Amazing stories)
Includes bibliographical references.
ISBN 1-55153-971-3

1. Horse stealing--Canada--History. I. Title. II. Series: Amazing stories
(Canmore, Alta.)

HV6665.C3P43 2003   364.16'2   C2003-906767-X

An application for the trademark for Amazing Stories™
has been made and the registered trademark is pending.

Printed and bound in Canada by Friesens
2 4 6 8 9 7 5 3

For Lambros, the *only* person who cared
to learn the truth, never abandoned me,
and gave a damn if I lived or died.

Contents

Prologue

It was 4:00 a.m. on October 28, 1915, and Saskatchewan farmer O.J. Mack rolled out of bed to begin the day's chores. Heading outside, Mack struggled to adjust his eyes to the darkness of early morning. As he squinted in the dimness, he noticed that his two horses were gone. At first he assumed his neighbours had let the horses out to pasture, but as daylight broke, he realized this wasn't the case. There, on the ground before him, were the very clear tracks of two horses and one human. Mack was certain the hoofprints belonged to his horses; he recognized one set as the uncertain step of his mare. She was blind.

With mounting anxiety, Mack followed his horses' hoofprints until they ended and a set of buggy tracks started. He followed the buggy tracks for the rest of the day before finally losing them. Distraught, he then returned to his farmhouse and reported his missing animals to the authorities. But what if the authorities couldn't get the horses back? What would he do then? Mack relied heavily on his strong, working horses for the proper functioning of his farm. Without them, the farm would be in trouble.

Stolen Horses

Days passed, and Mack heard nothing from the authorities. He began to fear that his horses would not be found alive and well. This fear only intensified when the Royal North-West Mounted Police finally contacted him. The news wasn't good. They needed him to come to headquarters to identify two horses that had been discovered lying dead in a coulee.

With sunken spirits, Mack steeled himself to look at the horse heads and other body parts that the staff sergeant had brought back with him from the scene. When Mack opened a box containing the severed, decomposing head of a stolen gelding, a wave of relief engulfed him. "That's not my horse," he said, exhaling slowly. Suddenly Mack felt a renewed sense of hope. Perhaps his horses would be found after all. Perhaps his farm could be saved, and the animals would be returned safely in the near future.

Then he opened the box containing the second head, and his heart sank. "That's my mare."

Chapter 1
Cross-Border Thefts

Throughout the 1800s, it was a known fact that the quality of Canada's livestock was much higher than that of the United States'. Unfortunately, this meant that Canadian horses were frequently stolen, taken across the border into the U.S., and sold to American aristocrats for top dollar.

In New York State, horse stealing and smuggling was a lucrative job for many scoundrels. In fact, by 1812, as Canadians and Americans became entrenched in war, stealing from frustrated farmers got to be so profitable in New York that some thieves had no other form of employment. Among the most ruthless of the horse thieves at that time were the leaders of the notorious Loomis Gang.

Stolen Horses

George Washington Loomis, father of the Loomis Gang, settled in Oneida County, New York, in 1802. Though he had reportedly been chased out of Vermont for horse stealing, George was nevertheless regarded as an educated, industrious, and respected farmer. The best livestock in the county belonged to him, and his fine horses were the envy of all. At the Oneida County family home, George and his wife raised 10 children — six sons and four daughters — and each of them seemed relatively bright and likeable. The entire family treated anyone who entered the Loomis home as a welcome guest.

But the six Loomis boys were far from the charming little things they pretended to be. They were troublemakers by nature, and, undoubtedly influenced by their own father's propensity for horse stealing, they soon matured into counterfeiters, liars, and thieves.

The oldest of the Loomis sons was William. Not the brightest of the brothers, he had a disagreeable disposition and was more a follower than a leader. The second oldest son, however, was a born leader. Described as unusually bright by a former schoolmaster, Washington "Wash" Loomis was keen, perceptive, and charismatic. His way with words enabled him to disarm enemies and convince potentially damaging witnesses to lie to authorities.

Grove Loomis, third oldest among the Loomis boys, lacked the verbal abilities of his older brother Wash. Grove was a fierce man, feared by everyone. The dubious owner of several purebred horses, he was an excellent horseman, capable of riding long distances over rough terrain. His brother Wheeler, fourth in line, was perhaps the worst scoundrel of the gang. The only family member who actually served time in the penitentiary, he was said to have "not a redeeming quality." Wheeler was the gang's official scout, and therefore directly responsible for many a stolen Canadian horse being led across the border.

The two youngest Loomis sons, Denio and Plumb, were unscrupulous, but lacked the artistry, imagination, and courage of their older brothers. Neither was trustworthy, and they were quick to abandon other gang members when things got tough. Though the brothers made up the core of the Loomis Gang, many other scoundrels joined forces with the group as well.

The Loomis Gang conducted business with the utmost efficiency. Usually working under cover of darkness, they would sneak across the border into Canada and go about their thieving. Everyone in the gang knew exactly where they were going, which farms to hit, and which horses they were after. Nighttime only lasted so long, and gang members couldn't waste time getting lost on trails or chasing down a broken old nag that would only fetch the going rate for horses. Every moment's delay increased the chance that a horse's rightful owner would wake up and rush out to defend his property.

In order to reduce the possibility of getting caught, gang

members tied pieces of burlap around the stolen horses' hooves to muffle the sound of their feet hitting the ground. Once the thieves gathered up the 60 to 70 horses they came to Canada to collect, they quickly made their way to Brockville, Ontario, and then back across the border, herding their investment all the way. During the summer months, flat-bottomed boats carried the bewildered horses across the St. Lawrence River.

When safely back on U.S. soil, the gang ushered the horses over flat land to Hammond, New York, and then on to the sparsely settled town of Rossie. By the time the horses arrived in the Rossie area, they were more than ready to rest in one of the town's many hiding places.

Early on in their criminal careers, the Loomis Gang chose the tiny town of Rossie as a main hideout and terminal for their stolen horses. Located in New York's St. Lawrence County, on the southern side of the St. Lawrence River, Rossie was an ideal location for a quick nip across the border to acquire some Canadian loot — namely healthy, strong, well-fed horses. The gang liked the fact that there wasn't much in the way of open terrain around Rossie. The area, with its dense overgrowth, many rocks, and muddy footing, was the perfect place for a bunch of horse thieves and their new-found horses to keep out of sight.

But the gang liked more than just the town's location and terrain. They also liked the fact that the impoverished townspeople were too busy trying to earn a living to bother reporting suspicious activity in the area. Life was tough in Rossie. People worked hard, but their standard of living remained far below that of the southern states. Most of the residents figured their lives were hard enough without inviting trouble by ratting on a bunch of horse thieves. And, those who might have felt the urge to talk to the local constabulary were usually paid for their silence.

Every once in a while, an honest, God-fearing resident would feel inclined to act on his conscience and report the gang's activities. But these residents would quickly learn that there was worse to fear than the wrath of God. Indeed, the Loomis Gang were better friends than enemies, and anyone who was fool enough to take them on would quickly find his house burned to the ground, his livestock stolen, his character assassinated, or some such similar catastrophe.

With the Loomis Gang's growing interest in the region, it didn't take long for Rossie to become the hub of horse thievery. As former Rossie historian, the late Virgie B. Simmons, once explained, "An early hotel keeper in the village said on many a dark night he heard the thud of horse's feet passing through the dust of the crooked road to Hammond. Once he counted sixty-five of them. I doubt if that number could be found in the whole town today."

The gang had several terminals throughout New York and other states in order to facilitate the distribution of their stolen horses. Their main terminal was a property in Rossie that they rented from a local farmer named Rastus Reynolds.

Stolen Horses

They soon rigged the farm with hiding places, trap doors, and secret escape hatches. Though Reynolds later realized that his property was being rented for ill use, the gold coins handed over to him persuaded the strapped farmer that horses were a much more profitable crop than corn.

The Reynolds farm was a desirable hideout for the Loomis Gang because the property had two hidden ways to get in and out. One was located at the southern end of the Indian River Bridge and the other was located just a few yards beyond. These access points led to secret trails that wound through rocky, untracked wilderness. The unknown trails were important to the gang for the expeditious and furtive movement of the horses.

The gang couldn't let the horses rest for long in Rossie. As soon as the animals were watered and deemed rested enough, they were back on the move. Gang members, always on the alert, barely had time to catch their own breath before they were herding the animals on trails that led from northerly points to the central part of New York. Many early homes, built well back from the roads, served as beacons for the gang. A light in a particular window of a select house along the "underground horse railroad" indicated it was safe for the gang to proceed. If there was no light shining, the gang took the horses to the nearest hideout and waited. Sometimes they holed up at prearranged safe houses or hid in forests for days at a time.

Though the Loomis brothers and the rest of the gang

needed to get the stolen horses out of their possession as quickly as possible, they were careful not to rush and get caught. They were also careful not to push the animals. Under Grove Loomis's direction, the thieves knew they couldn't run the animals too quickly or recklessly. The animals were a stolen investment, and if they died en route or arrived at the point of sale looking run-down and bearing cuts and injuries, then the investment would depreciate considerably. Gang members were knowledgeable horsemen and knew how to keep the animals in good flesh.

They also knew how to alter the appearance of various horses so that it was difficult for owners to recognize their own animals — even when they'd only lost them the night before. One team of horses was bought back by its original owner, who was unaware that he was purchasing his own stolen team! The gang used dyes, silver nitrate, and other chemicals to change the look of the vulnerable animals. Sometimes a hot baked potato was bound tightly to a horse's forehead to destroy the pigment of the hair, giving the horse the appearance of having a white star on its face. Such camouflage made it difficult to identify horses and consequently prove they had been stolen. Still, whether provable or not, everyone in northern New York knew what was going on.

The hidden trails the gang used ended at Utica, New York, the location of the closest railway to the southern states. If all went well, it usually took the gang three or four days to get to Utica, where the unsuspecting horses were loaded onto trains and shipped to wealthy buyers in the South.

Throughout much of the 1800s, the Loomis Gang dominated the horse-theft industry, growing rich off countless Canadian horses, as well as animals from other states. By 1813, authorities in Canada were making an effort to do something about these thefts. That year, Colonel Frazier and his company of British Regulars were sent to the United States to look for horse thieves. When they arrived in Rossie, they quickly surrounded the town's population of fewer than 500 people. Frazier vowed to put an end to the thievery. He then left his horse and some of his men at the Rossie Hotel, and went off with a small party to search for scoundrels. By morning, his horse had disappeared. While villagers rocked with laughter, troops scurried back to Canada. Up against the cunning Loomis brothers, the Regulars were completely out of their league!

Authorities were no match for the Loomis Gang. Although the brothers and other gang members were often arrested (for thievery, plundering, hiding a fugitive from lawmen, or any other number of offences), they were rarely convicted. No sooner were gang members placed in jail than a respectable person from the community would come to sign a bond to bail them out.

As the years passed, the gang's criminal ventures blossomed into a large-scale business due mostly to wealthy Southerners who bought the horses for high prices. The biggest market and most outrageous prices in the South were to be had during the Civil War (1861 to 1865), when the Confederate army desperately needed good artillery and cavalry horses, and paid handsomely for the stolen animals.

This pressing need for horses resulted not only in a booming business for the Loomis Gang, it also created a new career track for deserters from both the Union and Confederate armies. Men adopted horse stealing with the gusto of a businessman on an upwardly mobile career path. Even Canadians joined in the theft and re-sale market to the South.

As the market grew, gang members began to notice the growing competition they were facing. It took little effort for gang members to convince many of the deserters and renegades to join their ranks and form a syndicate, ingeniously removing the competition while increasing their market share. Thieves continued to sneak into Canada and steal the best horses on the northern side of the St. Lawrence, leaving frustrated Canadian farmers struggling to find replacement animals with which to bring in their crops or provide transportation.

Every once in a while, the Loomis Gang would head to Canada to sell a horse instead of steal one. On one occasion, a Canadian buyer even made money off the notorious gang! This unusual episode began when a new neighbour of the Loomis' called on them, as was the custom back then. After introducing himself to Wash Loomis, the neighbour explained that he was a man of little means, and that he hoped he could make his way through life without neighbour troubles. Wash, playing the role of country gentleman, assured the man that he, too, hoped to co-exist, and was even willing to look out for his neighbour's interests.

Not long after his conversation with Wash, the neighbour lost his best horse. A brave individual, he walked straight to the Loomis house and confronted Wash, reminding him of his promise. Wash denied any knowledge of the missing horse and, like a good neighbour, swore he would keep his eyes open for the animal.

Unbeknownst to Wash, some of the gang had, in fact, stolen the animal, taken him across the border to Canada, and sold him. When Wash discovered this was the case, he tracked the horse down and, even though it cost him a whopping $300 to do so, returned the horse to its rightful owner. After this, Wash and his neighbour had the utmost respect for each other's strength of character, and there were no more "incidents" between them.

Grove Loomis, however, had more difficulty staying out of trouble. In 1865, Grove offered to pay a local farmer $30 for a horse, but claimed he would have to take the animal to the next train station in order to get the money. When Grove returned, he nonchalantly informed the man that he was without horse or money. After many years of silently enduring the gang's exploits, this treachery was the last straw for local farmers and the gang's other victims.

On October 29, 1865, at the height of the family's

"career," Wash Loomis was duped into getting out of bed and leaving the house to respond to a man's whispered plea to come outside and speak to him. Upon stepping out the front door, Wash was promptly attacked by an angry mob of locals, his face beaten beyond recognition, his skull fractured. As he lay dying, the small mob, consisting of three men (including the local constable), went into the house in search of Grove. There were 14 other people asleep in the Loomis mansion at the time.

The constable stood outside Grove's bedroom door and told him that he had come for him. Believing that he was being arrested, Grove got out of bed and compliantly accompanied the constable downstairs, where he was beaten to a pulp. As he screamed, his attackers covered him with kerosene-soaked sacks and blankets and set him on fire. Despite suffering serious injuries Grove lived through the ordeal, thanks in large part to one of his sisters, who threw a coat over him to extinguish the flames.

Though Grove survived, the Loomis family spirit was broken, and the gang's activities ground to a halt. Grove retired to a small farm and died in 1877. As the years went by, the other brothers retired to the farming life and passed away one by one. Wheeler Loomis, the brother who spent most of his time living and scouting horses in Canada, died at Alexandria, Ontario, on March 20, 1911. His body was returned to the United States for burial, at which time Canadian horse-owners undoubtedly breathed easier.

Chapter 2
The British Remount

On September 15, 1906, a man named E.C. Johnson spotted his stolen horse at the Calgary stockyards. The animal was standing with 115 British remounts, all headed for Montreal on the first leg of a voyage to South Africa. Johnson, eager to have his horse back, notified Superintendent R. Burton Dean of the Royal North-West Mounted Police (RNWMP) about the animal. But in the time it took Deane to confirm Johnson's claim, the horse in question had been loaded onto an eastbound train with the other remounts.

Recognizing the need for swift action, Deane immediately instructed one of his sergeants to find out who had sold the horse to the British government, but to "make [the] enquiries secretly so as not to give the thief warning." He then notified RNWMP Commissioner A.B. Perry about the situation. Before the sun set that night, Perry issued a telegram to Staff Sergeant M.V. Gallivan in Winnipeg: "One of the British remounts is alleged to have been stolen from E.C. Johnson, Calgary." Following a description of the animal, the telegram closed with, "If horse found answering this description detain it."

The train carrying the remounts was scheduled to stop at Winnipeg for refuelling, and when it did, Gallivan was standing on the railway platform, waiting to inspect the animals. He promptly found the horse and seized it on authority of Commissioner Perry's order.

Meanwhile, back in Calgary, Superintendent Deane had tracked down the horse trader who had sold the horse to the British government. The trader, George Hoadley, told Deane that he had purchased the horse the previous spring from a man named Charles MacDonald. Hoadley also acknowledged that the brands on his horse and those on the allegedly stolen horse were identical. But he insisted that the horse he had sold had been troublesome to ride, while Johnson claimed that his horse had been gentle. This appeared to be the only discrepancy between the horses. Hoadley, concerned at being implicated in horse theft, invited Johnson to talk with him — presumably to convince him that the purchase of the horse had been legal.

Two days after spotting his stolen horse, Johnson spoke

with Hoadley on the telephone at the RNWMP station in Calgary. By the time Johnson hung up the phone, he was convinced that Hoadley had, in fact, owned the horse legally, and he dropped his claim. A police sergeant also confirmed Hoadley's lawful ownership and deciphered that MacDonald had branded all his horses in the same manner. Two of these horses, which he had sold to two different buyers (Johnson and Hoadley), had been similar in appearance. The matter, it seemed, was settled.

Upon hearing this latest development, Superintendent Deane sent word to Commissioner Perry, asking him to arrange for "disposal of horse." But the commissioner could not comply; his authority was limited to sending the animal back to its owner. Suddenly, telegrams were flying back and forth as the RNWMP and other officials tried to arrange for the horse to rejoin the remounts. One of these telegrams indicated that the other 115 remounts had left Winnipeg bound for Montreal the same day that the complaint had been filed. It would be impossible to send the horse on by itself. Upon hearing this news, Commissioner Perry grew concerned. "This matter will justly cause much complaint," he predicted. He had no idea just how right he was.

Now the RNWMP had to figure out what to do with the horse they had seized. Wanting to solve the problem as quickly as possible, Superintendent Deane asked Johnson if he would take ownership of horse, seeing as it resembled his missing horse so closely. But Johnson conceded ownership to

Hoadley. Evidently he didn't want just any old horse, he wanted his own horse. Disappointed, Deane notified the commissioner: "British Government is admittedly now the owner."

The British army agent who had purchased the horse from Hoadley got involved. Unfavourably impressed, and afraid that his purchase might reflect badly on him, the agent began demanding that the RNWMP — or somebody — pay the expenses incurred for the army's loss of the horse. He demanded a lot of things, including payment for the vacant stall on the ship that had just left Montreal. Superintendent Deane complained to Commissioner Perry, "it is not easy to get him to talk reasonably on the subject." Then he restated the commissioner's fears. "No doubt the matter will be the subject of considerable complaint, but the police could surely have done nothing else than they did."

The British army did not agree. When British Colonel Charles H. Bridge, Inspector of Remounts, learned of the seized horse on September 21, 1906, he was livid. He immediately wired the commissioner: "I am now writing and demanding a refund of the sum paid for the horse. Of course the horse will now be of no use to the Imperial Government, even should the allegation of theft prove unfounded...You may however think it right to enquire into the circumstances attending the seizure of a horse merely alleged to be stolen."

Apparently, Colonel Bridge thought the allegedly stolen horse should have been allowed to continue the journey to Montreal and board the steamer bound for South Africa. But the RNWMP knew they would have come under severe criticism if they had permitted such a thing and then found out that the horse had indeed been stolen.

In such an event, would Colonel Bridge, or anyone else for that matter, have taken the animal out of service and returned it, by ship from South Africa, to its rightful owner? In such circumstances, the British army may have been considered party to the theft. But Bridge regarded the police seizure of the horse as akin to theft from the government, and the tone of his letter signalled what was to come.

As the RNWMP and British army tossed the horse's fate back and forth, it became abundantly clear how the mounties earned their respected reputation around the world. Those early lawmen were truly dedicated. They took great pride in doing the right thing, and were prepared to make the necessary effort to bring it to pass.

Throughout his communications with the police, Colonel Bridge's chief complaint seemed to be that he had not been personally notified of the seizure, but had found out about it five days after the fact from a foreman.

As the mess got murkier, the Secretary of the Territorial Live Stock Association C.W. Peterson, got into the fray. He was required to look after the horse until the fate of the animal was determined. A rather forceful fellow, it took all the RNWMP's patience and devotion to duty to communicate politely with him. He referred to the RNWMP as simply the NWM Police, disregarding the honour bestowed on the force in 1904 by King Edward VII, when, in recognition of service to the Crown, the law enforcement agency was given the "Royal" prefix. "The horse is now on our hands as a result of this idiotic blunder," Peterson wrote. He vehemently demanded that legal action be taken against the original complainant, Johnson.

But Johnson couldn't be faulted. There was no evidence of malicious intent on his part, nor did it seem that he had made the claim of theft recklessly. The horses had been almost identical, and an honest mistake had been made.

By September 24, the Department of Militia and Defence in Ottawa had received a letter from Bridge, which described the seizure of the horse and accused the RNWMP of being "high-handed." Wanting to address this matter quickly, the department contacted Lieutenant Colonel Fred White, Comptroller for the RNWMP, to make him aware of the letter. "No doubt the seizure of the horse was all correct," White was told, "but it would seem that immediate notice ought to have been sent to its then owner, especially as he was a Government official purchasing for the British Government. It occurred to [the department] that perhaps you ought to know of this."

As early as September 26, Lawrence Fortescue, filling in for Fred White, sent a handwritten note to Commissioner Perry in Regina suggesting that the best plan would be for the police to take ownership of the horse, purchasing it from the "Imperial Army."

He then requested that Perry give him a full report on the case. Commissioner Perry was not amused. He replied to Fortescue, "My Dear Fortescue: I have your semi-official letter … I have nothing to say in the matter."

The same day that Perry wrote to Fortescue, Colonel Bridge sent another telegraph to Ottawa. "Will accept one hundred and sixty dollars for horse. Am leaving for England and can ill spare time personal interview. No wish to dispute your opinion as to legality of seizure." Officials in Ottawa breathed a collective sigh of relief. All they had to do now was sign a cheque, and then they could finally close the file!

But remarkably, almost 100 more notes, letters, and telegrams were to pass between the police and army brass before the matter was resolved. On October 4, Lieutenant Colonel White sent a telegram to Commissioner Perry, repeating Fortescue's suggestion that the RNWMP buy the horse. This time Perry replied, "Quite willing to take over horse."

Upon receiving Perry's approval, White sent another telegram to Colonel Bridge: "If it will be a convenience to you we will take over horse held at Winnipeg, we repaying you purchase price."

It looked as though a settlement was close at hand. But for unknown reasons, it took Bridge three days to reply to White's note, and when he did so, he changed his previous offer: "Impossible to now take delivery of horse seized Winnipeg but I claim his purchase price plus all expenses."

He followed the telegram with a handwritten letter in which he complained at length about not having been notified directly about the horse's detainment. In the letter he also asked that his Canadian agents be contacted to arrange the settlement.

Not through yet, Bridge then undertook an action that conveyed his fierce determination to be reimbursed in full, to the penny: he contacted a law firm. His lawyers proceeded to write a menacing letter to the RNWMP. From the mounties' perspective, it was a dirty, underhanded thing to do under the circumstances, but they showed admirable restraint.

With a level head, Lieutenant Colonel White wrote a lengthy reply to Bridge. "It is scarcely necessary to remind you, with your knowledge and experience, that combinations for the illegal possession of horse flesh are always active, and it is only by prompt action on the part of the Police — sometimes on vague information — that horse stealing is kept in check, a condition not limited to Canada. You seem to feel injured that direct communication was not made to you of the seizure of this particular horse. Now from my point of view I think the proper person to notify you was your Agent who had charge of the animals."

White gently, but firmly, put things in perspective while maintaining a dignified stance. "I trust you will concede that the Police did all that was reasonable under the circumstances," he concluded, reminding Colonel Bridge that the RNWMP had offered to buy the horse for use in the police mounted unit, but had not received a clear response in the affirmative or otherwise.

The letter proved effective. Bridge immediately contacted his Canadian agent and told him that White was willing to buy the horse and pay his expenses, and that he approved of the offer. But, not quite able to be as affable as White, Bridge added, "unless you think matter gone too far."

Just when it looked like the horse had found a rather enviable home, Bridge had brought everything to a halt again so that his agent could decide if the matter had "gone too far." During this delay, officials from the Canadian Pacific Railway (CPR) appeared on the scene. They were holding the RNWMP responsible for horse-related costs. It is almost unbelievable that this horse could unwittingly cause so many people such a painful headache for such a long time. (One can only wonder what impact it's gentle twin had on the world at large!)

The RNWMP waited to hear from Bridge's Canadian agent. And continued to wait. Frustrated by the ridiculous delay, Superintendent Deane went into action once more. He discovered that the agent had changed employers. Deane quickly tracked him down in hopes of doing damage control. By now everyone was squirming at the bureaucratic mess that had evolved.

Deane learned that when Bridge had asked the agent to let him know if the matter had gone too far, the agent had replied with a telegram the same day. "Let Police take horse," he'd said. But the telegram had not been delivered. In fact, it had completely disappeared. Had that message been delivered, the matter would have been closed in late October. But without the telegram, one of the most frustrating horse theft investigations in the history of the RNWMP had been stalled yet again.

Once Deane tracked down Bridge's ex-agent, it was full steam ahead one more time. Commissioner Perry personally instructed Gallivan to make the best possible arrangements for the horse, as it was being acquired for use in the mounted unit.

Everyone wanted this case closed. White worked quickly, getting statements and signatures and paying bills before another wrench could be thrown into the mix. The purchase price of the horse was $160. The CPR submitted a transport requisition for $20. The RNWMP also paid out $40.05 for the horse's keep while it was detained in Winnipeg. In all, costs totalled $220.05 — almost double the normal price for a police horse.

Perry, despite complaining about someone else issuing the requisition for the animal's care, attributed the mammoth expense of the dozens of telegrams that had been exchanged to "ordinary" police expenditures.

Petty complaints and requests for signatures verifying small expenses continued to be exchanged among officials. The most blatant "dig" came from White himself, in a letter to the War Office in London, England. Detailing the expenses incurred, he stated, "It is a case of having to pay dearly for a friendly, but unappreciated, effort to assist another branch of the public service." He then promptly wrote his closing salutation: "I have the honour to be, Sir, Your obedient servant."

White sent the correspondence and then informed the clerk of the Privy Council in Ottawa that the horse had been purchased for $160. On May 1, 1907, White received a reply from the War Office in England, thanking him for payment received and stating, "I am to add that the Army Council regret the trouble and expense which have fallen upon your department in connection with this matter."

With the closing of this amazing case, one has to ponder the influence it had on the nameless horse. Although most horses come out of theft situations worse off than they went into them, this is definitely one case where the horse benefited from being thought stolen. Even if the animal had survived the gruelling journey to South Africa, the Boer War had not been long over, and it's doubtful what kind of life the animal would have had. Instead, the horse gave its life to the service of honourable men, and their admirable Force.

Chapter 3
Tracking Jack Anderson

On July 20, 1915, 27-year-old J.C. Clark gathered some camping gear and a .22 rifle, hitched his buggy to a couple of horses, and left the farm where his mother and brother were living. With several theft convictions under his belt and a string of failed jobs behind him, he was more than ready to fulfill his entrepreneurial spirit.

Clark had immigrated to Canada from England in the early 1900s. He stood about five feet, 10 inches tall, and had a mouth filled with decaying teeth. His dark brown hair, parted down the centre of his head, was allowed to grow long in the front to cover a scar on his right temple. The scar was the result of a horse's hoof making forceful contact with his head

— perhaps that was when Clark began to think differently.

The evening after he left his mother and brother, Clark halted his horses at the top of a hill near Assiniboia, Saskatchewan, and surveyed the countryside. As he took in the view, he saw eight head of horses at pasture, and among them, two Clydesdale mares with their foals. The two mares were grazing contentedly, one with a yearling filly nearby, the other with a suckling colt. Quick as a flash, Clark harnessed the two mares to a brand-new democrat buggy that was parked close by and with the two youngsters in tow, ran the horses south at a fast pace.

Tucked in the southeast corner of Saskatchewan, Assiniboia is located about 80 kilometres from the Montana border and 180 kilometres from the North Dakota border. Though tempted by his proximity to Montana, Clark knew that as soon as word got out that the Clydesdales and their foals had been stolen, authorities would be waiting for them at the nearby border. He decided to take the longer route to North Dakota, stopping along the way to visit an acquaintance named Ernest Counce, who lived near Viceroy, Saskatchewan.

By his own admission, Counce had been a lifelong crook, but he had settled at his present abode in an attempt to escape his old acquaintances and turn his life to the good. Unfortunately, Counce found that his old associates were happy to follow him, just to maintain friendly ties. When Clark arrived, he wanted something to eat, and Counce generously provided breakfast for both him and a hired hand by the name of Jack Anderson.

When breakfast was over, Clark led Counce and Anderson to the northeast side of Counce's pasture. There, standing in a coulee just beyond the property, were the four stolen horses and the democrat buggy. Clark and Anderson hid the buggy, hobbled the mares in some nearby bushes, then hogtied the foals and set about making them look older.

Soon after, Clark took the two mares to North Dakota. By crossing the border into the United States, he was immediately guilty not just of horse theft, but of smuggling as well. The closest settlement in North Dakota was Fortuna, and Clark tried to unload the horses to a resident named John Lenniger for a mere $250. Lenniger wasn't sure that he liked the look of Clark, and he asked straight out if the mares were Clark's to sell.

"I got them from my brother-in-law, William Card, of Rudser," Clark lied.

Clark had only been in Fortuna for three days when he discovered that Lenniger had sent someone to verify his information. Immediately, Clark took his leave, scuttling off with the two mares and desperately trying to sell them to anyone he encountered. He got as far as Crosby, North Dakota, where he was arrested and charged with smuggling Clydesdales into the United States.

Meanwhile, a Royal North-West Mounted Police Officer named Detective Sergeant Reames had been making inquiries about the stolen horses in Saskatchewan's Viceroy District. In early August of 1915, he was sent to Crosby, North Dakota, to ascertain whether the horses Clark had had in his possession at the time of his arrest were those belonging to Mr. Woods of Assiniboia. If they were, Reames was to ensure that extradition proceedings were commenced.

Reames made a positive identification of J.C. Clark, and then looked over the weary mares. One had a serious rope burn on her right forefoot — the result of being hobbled. "This team has evidently been travelled very fast recently and were almost done up," Reames noted. He determined that the mares closely resembled the description of Mr. Woods's horses. He laid a charge against Clark, under the North Dakota Criminal Code, for having stolen the mares in Divide County, North Dakota. Though this charge was not accurate, U.S. law allowed that horses stolen in any county, state, or country could be declared as having been stolen in the county in which the offender was arrested. As Reames later explained, "The charge ... was laid merely to hold Clark on until the owner of the team could be gotten to Crosby to identify them."

News of Clark's arrest reached Counce and Anderson a week later by way of a letter sent from Clark himself. The minute Anderson read the letter, he moved into high gear. "He lit out with the two colts for Montana," claimed Counce.

Indeed, Anderson took off so quickly that Counce, left behind, didn't see the law coming for *him* through the dust.

Sure enough, Counce was arrested and remanded for 16 days, pending further investigation. Meanwhile, Clark escaped from custody in North Dakota. Without the luxury of time, he was unable to select a decent riding horse to steal, and had to settle for the first animal he came across — an old, tired horse with visible injuries to its legs and feet. Somehow, the animal got Clark to Counce's farm where, in Counce's absence, Clark holed up for a couple of days. Then, like most men on the run, Clark became nervous that the law would sneak up on him, so he moved on to his brother's farm.

By the time he got out of jail, Counce was furious. He hadn't appreciated being incarcerated, especially as he'd been trying so hard to go straight. He was still licking his wounds when Clark, carefully avoiding authorities, made his way back to Counce's house and knocked on the door. Much to Counce's annoyance, Clark hung around, hoping that Anderson would show up.

After a couple of days, Clark left, only to return a month later, still on the run. Wanting Clark out of his life for good, Counce ordered him to leave. "You're no damned good," he yelled, "you got me into trouble once and you're a black bungler!"

Clark left, but returned again a month later, still wanting very much to get in touch with Anderson. This time, he was at Counce's less than three hours when Anderson arrived with a buggy and team.

Anderson and Clark left the next day for Montana,

where they went into big-time horse stealing, having as many as six stolen horses on hand at any one time. They enlisted the services of other horse thieves, and before long, their band of criminals was enjoying a fair deal of notoriety. The group stole and sold horses throughout Montana, North Dakota, and southern Saskatchewan. They hid the horses at the farms of friends or relatives until the animals could be unloaded. And they cared not one toss about the welfare of the animals.

On October 28, 1915, Clark and Anderson went on a stealing spree. They stole three horses from a pasture near Avonlea, Saskatchewan, and then went on to take two large horses from a barn 11 kilometres to the south. The two large horses, belonging to a farmer named O.J. Mack, were stunningly flashy and handsome. When Clark and Anderson went to hide the animals near Counce's farm, Counce warned the men that they'd never be able to sell the two large horses because they were so identifiable. Unconcerned, Anderson responded, "I'll soon ditch them."

In December of 1915, Clark returned to Counce's farm on two occasions. The first time, he arrived with a couple of horses that Counce recognized as belonging to a neighbour only a few kilometres away; the next time, he turned up with a team of horses that impressed Counce so much he offered to buy them — an offer that Clark cunningly refused. The men became embroiled in an altercation over the team, and Clark left, telling Counce's wife that he couldn't stand her husband any longer.

Months later, on March 30, 1916, Anderson showed up at Counce's place while Counce was away. Mrs. Counce, however, was still at home, and it wasn't long before she and Anderson were frolicking in the hayloft. The new couple planned to ride off into the sunset together the next time Anderson left for Montana. But for now, Anderson was content to enjoy the warm days of summer at Counce's homestead.

One night, after Counce and his wife had an argument, Anderson decided to make his move. In no time, he and Mrs. Counce were headed to the Montana border, with Clark tagging along as babysitter to Counce's two children. "He stole those that were nearest and dearest to me," Counce later said of Anderson.

Around this time, the RNWMP was beginning to dedicate serious manpower to its investigation of Anderson and Clark. Still trying to leave his life of crime behind, and also wanting revenge, Counce revealed all he knew about the thieves to Staff Sergeant Mundy, who had been assigned as lead investigator on the case. Counce also filled Mundy in on the latest news about the two beautiful mares that had been stolen from O.J. Mack. "I am since informed that they are laying dead in a coulee, with bullet holes through their heads," Counce said.

When he discovered the fate of the horses, Mundy was required to gather evidence. "I got possession of the heads of the two beasts, as well as portions of the hides, where brands and scars should be, and enough of the leg to show peculiarities," he reported. He then took the heads, legs, and hide samples to Assiniboia so that they might be preserved as court evidence.

As Mundy continued to gather evidence against the thieves, Clark and Anderson set up house in Montana with Counce's little missus. When Clark's company was no longer welcome — perhaps because he'd done some furtive bungling around the house — Anderson gave him his marching orders. Then Anderson made an honest woman out of Mrs. Counce and — legally or otherwise — she became Mrs. Anderson. In no time, the Andersons were parents to two additional children.

With his large family to feed, Anderson felt the need to further expand his horse thieving business. His band snatched animals from the Glasgow area of Montana, and sold many just south of the Saskatchewan border at Scobey. As the thieving continued, the pile of stolen horse complaints on the Glasgow sheriff's desk grew higher.

Meanwhile, Mundy was still discretely sniffing around, trying to get evidence against Anderson and Clark that would hold up in court. To prevent word reaching the crooks that a policeman was making inquiries, Mundy presented himself as a livestock insurance agent to any potential witnesses. He gave the following report to his superiors:

News travels very quickly between Crooks of this kind

... if extradition is to be asked for, the applications must be rushed through, in order that the chase may be taken up not later than Wednesday or Thursday of this week ... one thing I am sure of, and that is that there is no use relying upon the officials in Valley County or Phillipps County to locate [Anderson and Clark]. It is a question of us going over the ground ourselves ... and if possible, taking with us a man specially sworn in at Glasgow, to effect arrest, a man that is not known as a deputy. To do this may entail considerable time and expense, and will require the work of two men, with full privilege to act as appears best to them ... Corporal Worgan of Ogema knows Anderson and Clarke. He is a reliable man in a tight corner, and if I am to go on the work, I would specially ask that he be detailed in plain clothes and that a purely civilian outfit be supplied us. This should consist of team, and democrat, saddle horse, small tent and camp outfit, rifles.

Inspector Denis Ryan, Mundy's superior officer, concurred with Mundy's recommendations. He was still sore at U.S. law enforcement for letting Clark escape custody after they'd nabbed him in North Dakota for the theft of the Clydesdale horses. Ryan appealed to the commanding officer of the Regina District of the RNWMP, noting that Clark and Anderson were "notorious horse thieves, and a menace to the stock-owners of this Province, I therefore beg to recommend that no expense be spared to capture them."

Were it not for the fact that so many people were willing

to give the crooks a hiding place and warn them of police movement, the expense factor may have been much less of a police worry. But with this kind of help from civilians, Anderson and his band of thieves were becoming increasingly cocky, reckless, and dangerous. The RNWMP was eager to stop the stealing, and Mundy gave the case his undivided attention.

On September 4, 1916, Mundy found Clark and Anderson in Billings, Montana. The two thieves were involved with a man who was about to ship 150 head of horses into Canada to sell to the unwary. As Mundy continued to work incognito, almost single-handedly gathering evidence, he became concerned about whether or not fellow lawmen in the area would bungle his case. "I know of my own experience that the Deputy Sheriff at Zootman, one Riley Brooks, is a crook of the first order, the Sheriff of Phillips County is nearly as bad, and that to use either of those men on our work, would spell certain failure. They do not do their duty, that's all there is to it," he reported.

The RNWMP took Mundy's concerns to heart, and as he got closer to making an arrest, his superiors assigned him the help of another lawman, and a car — which promptly broke down three kilometres from the Montana ranch that Mundy planned to use as a home base. His new partner took the car to be repaired while Mundy headed to the ranch on foot.

The ranch was located close to Anderson's farm, and Mundy stopped for a while to stake out the thief's property.

Tracking Jack Anderson

Through his binoculars, he saw Anderson drive up to the farmhouse and go inside. When no one came out of the house, Mundy started back to the ranch, planning to have supper and return after dark to raid the Anderson property. But before he reached the ranch, he unexpectedly came across a cache of three fillies and two grown mares, one of which had a suckling foal. The mares were harnessed and hobbled; the foal was badly cut up from wire fencing, so exhausted that it lay flat out on the ground, unable to move.

Knowing time was of the essence, Mundy walked quickly on to the ranch, where he hoped to find a horse that he could use for transportation. A hired hand was there with an old mare that he'd been riding all day. She was stiff and slow, with tender feet. Hoping another horse would become available soon, Mundy decided to prepare himself some grub and wait. But before he was able to finish his supper, he spotted, through his binoculars, someone riding in the direction of the cached horses. He rushed out the door and hoisted himself onto the old mare; the other rider spotted him and immediately picked up the pace.

Mundy rode straight for the rider, and when there were about 90 metres between them, he pointed his rifle and yelled, "Stop in the name of the RNWMP!" The rider uttered something unintelligible and continued on. Both horses were going full tilt. Mundy fired a warning shot in the air and then aimed at the rider's horse. As he did so, the old mare he was riding stumbled and somersaulted, and Mundy landed hard on the parched ground. The rider continued over the hills. Mundy remounted and followed. He got within about 350 metres then jumped off the mare, took steady aim, and fired five shots. Watching them ride off into the darkness, he saw the rider's horse begin to limp.

Positive that the rider was Anderson, Mundy returned to the cached horses and waited. When no one came for the animals, he and the old mare drove them to the nearby ranch for safety. Then he returned to the Anderson property to watch the house. The night was dark, and thick fog hid the moon. Mundy waited all night, but nobody came to the property or left it.

Just as the sun began to rise, Mundy snuck up to the house and pulled a one-man raid. He found Anderson's wife inside, but she claimed to be home alone, insisting that no one but the mailman had been to the house for days. Mundy, however, didn't overlook the fact that the dinner table, which hadn't been cleared, was set for three people.

Frustrated, Mundy left Mrs. Anderson and returned to the ranch. He had no idea who owned the horses he had taken under care, but was convinced they were stolen. Afraid that Anderson would return to re-steal them — he'd been bold enough to steal horses that were court exhibits against him — Mundy sent the animals to the police pasture at Swift Current, where he knew they'd be well cared for until their owner claimed them.

While Mundy continued to stake out the Anderson

house, another 40 head of horses was stolen nearby. "People here carry on their stock raising in fear and trembling of the Anderson gang," he reported.

On October 6, 1916, Counce gave another statement to police in which he identified several of Anderson's hiding places and suggested that these were the places where Mundy might look for him. "Anderson, Clark and Sparks (a cohort of Anderson's) are always aware of the police being in the vicinity and know just what is going on at all times," said Counce. "The only way to catch Anderson is to lie in wait for him at one of these caches, or for a couple of men to wait at each cache, and get him as the other people are succouring, because he pulls out in the early hours of the morning."

Counce's information, coupled with information that Mundy had obtained from two Montana constables, set the groundwork for arrests. "I learned that Sparks had recently driven a team to death," reported Mundy. Two days after these horses were stolen just south of Swift Current, they were driven to death, dying on the banks of a creek, where they were left. "I came here with my informant and this morning went over and examined the horses, one of them a mare and the other a gelding," said Mundy. The men pulled the gelding out of the creek and found it answered the description of the stolen gelding. "If the owner identified this horse, the possession of it by Sparks here can be proven by several witnesses, we can then tie Sparks up, and that will be the key-note to the whereabouts of Anderson," explained Mundy.

Sure enough, Mundy's plan worked. On October 11, 1916, the night guard on duty in Regina received a handwritten telegram for Superintendent McGibbon of the RNWMP. The sender was Mundy, in Montana, and the message read: "[Anderson and Ed Sparks] under arrest here to-night hurry along extradition papers both temporarily held on American warrants."

Clark was not arrested; he had disappeared. But with the other arrests began a mountain of paperwork required to get the scoundrels sent back to Canada to stand trial. Adding emphasis to the importance of the extraditions, Mundy informed his superior officer that there was approximately 35 head of horses loose on Anderson's range. Mundy was holding 13 head. "Shall I have balance rounded up?" he asked.

The RNWMP took a flood of depositions from those who'd had their horses stolen, as well as from Counce and other witnesses. By then, the circumstances of many of the victims were serious. O.J. Mack was visibly impoverished. He had used his horses every day to toil his fields. His situation was so dire that a police report on his ability to attend Anderson's preliminary hearing said: "From the appearance of his farm and surroundings I would judge that he is in very poor circumstances and not at all in a position to pay his own way." Police paid for Mack's transportation to the hearing so that he could be a witness and help put Anderson in jail.

Anderson and his gang would have continued to wreak havoc on other people's lives and horses while remaining untouched by the law had it not been for the work of RNWMP Staff Sergeant Mundy, and the significant aid he received from Ernest Counce. Both settlers and horses suffered when horses were stolen, and it took the courage of men like Counce, and the bravery and competence of men like Mundy, to bring them relief through justice.

Chapter 4
Name That Crook

On October 7, 1915, a telegram was sent to the Shaunavon, Saskatchewan detachment of the Royal North-West Mounted Police. A constable was needed immediately in Scotsguard, about 24 kilometres away as the crow flies. Constable Perry set out for Scotsguard the following morning, and soon met up with the telegram's sender, a Mr. Remackell. Though Remackell himself had not been involved in any illegal conduct, he was aware of some, and had taken it upon himself to alert the police. According to Remackell, Ted Williams, an employee of the Scotsguard Livery Barn, had disclosed that he'd stolen a couple of horses and had subsequently sold them to an unsuspecting farmer by the name of Harry Bolleson.

Name That Crook

Since then, Williams had last been seen walking in a southerly direction, away from town.

Constable Perry searched the Scotsguard area but was unable to locate Williams or anyone answering his description. However, as he gathered bits of information from several locals, he began to suspect that Williams was actually Art Smith, a thief whom authorities were already chasing. Perry returned to Shaunavon and picked up some WANTED posters that showed a picture Smith. He then returned to Scotsguard and showed the posters to the locals. Several people recognized the man in the picture as Ted Williams. Constable Perry now knew one of Smith's aliases. The WANTED poster also described the bay-coloured horse that Smith had last been seen riding. As it turned out, the horse's description matched perfectly with one of the animals sold to Bolleson.

Further investigation on Constable Perry's part revealed that Smith had arrived in Scotsguard with the two stolen horses on September 6, 1915. He had simply ridden in one day on a slim, branded, bay gelding, his hips rocking gently to the rhythm of the horse's stride. He was all dressed up in a brown and black mackinaw coat, pigskin boots, and a felt hat, and he led another horse: a smaller, grey gelding with a dark mane and tail. This horse wasn't branded, but it had a split on its left front hoof that was bad enough for people to notice.

Soon after his arrival in Scotsguard, Smith got a job at

the livery barn. Within a month, he revealed to two men who also worked there that he had stolen the bay horse from another livery barn in Harlem, Montana. He also let it be known that Mr. Bolleson had purchased the two horses for $100.

"I got these horses from a ranch down south," Smith had told Bolleson. "They've been working all summer long. They're a good pair and well worth the $100, sir."

After having looked them over, Bolleson had reached into his pocket and produced $100, for which Smith then provided a clear bill of sale. Of course, he'd signed the bill of sale "Ted Williams." Poor Bolleson. He'd lost $100 and hadn't even known that he should have been stunned.

Constable Perry knew that if Smith was crooked enough to steal horses, he was probably guilty of other crimes as well. An additional mountie, Constable J.H. Birks, was assigned to the case. Birks discovered that Smith had recently swindled another Scotsguard resident: he had sold a stolen saddle to Robert Stevenson. With the money from this sale, plus that of the horses, Smith went on a shopping spree, buying himself new pants, boots, and a cap.

After learning that Smith was still in the Scotsguard area, it wasn't long before Constable Birks tracked him down at the livery barn and arrested him. Following the arrest, Birks requested a remand, and Smith found himself confined to the guardroom in Maple Creek, Saskatchewan, for eight days while Birks gathered evidence for his trial. But when

Birks made his way across the border to gather much of this evidence, he soon learned that Smith's movements in the United States were not so easy to trace.

While he was in the U.S., Smith had done his best to conceal his activities and confuse anyone trying to follow his trail. He may not have been overly smart, but he was cunning. So cunning, in fact, that in the months leading up to his arrest, he'd managed to involve two teenagers from Shaunavon in his crime sprees on both sides of the border.

These teenagers were Bernard Madden and Perrine Hitchcock, friends whose fathers each owned homesteads in the Shaunavon area. In mid June of 1915, months before Smith's arrest, Madden and Hitchcock embarked on a trip to Harlem, Montana. Madden was in search of cattle to purchase for his dad's herd, and Hitchcock was looking for land.

Around the same time that Madden and Hitchcock were preparing for their trip south, Art Smith was making the acquaintance of a man named Charles Marsh at a Native camp near Harlem. Smith asked Marsh for a ride into Harlem, and Marsh obliged. Marsh's slender four-year-old bay horse carried both men the 20 kilometres into town. That night, the horse disappeared.

On June 16, Madden and Hitchcock rode into Harlem and put their horses in the livery barn. While there, they met the barn's newest employee: Art Smith. Hitchcock was immediately drawn to Smith. He hung around with the horse thief all evening and for most of the following day. Madden, however, had no desire to spend all his time in a livery barn; he left Hitchcock at the barn, paid a visit to the pool hall, and then went to see a movie.

When the movie ended (at about 9:00 p.m.), Madden and Hitchcock met up, as arranged, and left town. Madden rode his horse and Hitchcock walked alongside him, leading his own horse. After travelling about two kilometres, Hitchcock said, "I ain't walking any more. There's a train coming close by soon. I'm taking the train." He then took the saddle and bridle off his horse and set the animal free in a nearby pasture.

Madden couldn't help but notice that Hitchcock had found himself a pretty swanky saddle. He noticed it because his own was old and long past its prime. In fact, it was broken and thoroughly uncomfortable to ride in, but Madden and his father were unable to justify buying a new one when more cattle were needed first.

With Hitchcock gone, Madden rode on towards Willesden, North Dakota, alone. Not expecting to see anyone again before dawn, he was surprised after a couple of hours to hear the sound of hooves beating against the ground. They were moving fast and getting closer. Suddenly, out of the dark came Hitchcock, riding a buckskin horse with a brand on its left thigh. Behind him was Smith, riding a bay gelding.

"I changed my mind," Hitchcock said when he caught up to Madden. "Why pay for the train when you can ride a horse?"

"Where'd you get the horses?" asked Madden.

The two men smiled. "We got 'em."

Suspicious, Madden eyed the men and animals.

"What's the matter? You think we can't get horses when we need 'em?"

Not knowing what to say, young Madden let the subject drop.

For about a week, the trio cruised around the countryside. When they were just east of Grass Range, Montana, Hitchcock decided to trade horses with the only storekeeper in town. In exchange for the stolen gelding, Hitchcock received a bay mare. Smith also made a few trades, and the three men resumed their hobo lifestyle, riding past small towns in Montana and North Dakota, and leaving a string of theft victims in their wake.

In Beach, North Dakota, Hitchcock traded his horse again, this time for one owned by the milkman. Madden, following Hitchcock's lead, decided to trade his horse, too. He swapped animals with the mailman at Beach, ending up with a black, branded gelding with a bald face. The animal was so conspicuous that it would have been easy to pick it out in a line-up. Clearly, Madden was not cut out for a life of crime.

The men rode on to New England, North Dakota, where Hitchcock traded horses again. The bay mare he had been riding became a bay gelding — all that appeared to change was the horse's sex, but Hitchcock knew a sex change could make a witness's testimony worthless.

The men moved like rabbits, zigzagging and backtracking in order to conceal their activities and confuse anyone who might be trying to construct a sequence of events. During their travels, Smith, the leader of the trio, left the other two for days at a time. Madden and Hitchcock, however, stuck together, and Madden was present for each and every one of the horse trades Hitchcock made.

Before leaving New England, North Dakota, Hitchcock acquired a grey gelding from a young hotel worker, then he and Madden slowly headed back to Canada, crossing the border just southeast of Assiniboia, Saskatchewan. It was after dark when they arrived, about 10:00 p.m., and neither of them reported to Assiniboia customs.

Smith rejoined the two younger men, and the group made its way to the Scotsguard Livery Barn, where Hitchcock swapped his grey gelding for a young horse that needed to be broke and trained in order to be ridden — definitely not the most expeditious method of staying one step ahead of police! By this point, Madden, his mind reeling from all the horse swaps, left Smith and Hitchcock at the livery barn and went home.

Meanwhile, the liveryman, a fellow by the name of John Nordell, took Smith and Hitchcock into to his home and fed them supper. During the meal, Hitchcock told Nordell that he had got himself into "bad trouble" and that he'd "got the horse." Instead of contacting the authorities with this information, Nordell permitted Hitchcock to keep the stolen horse in his livery barn, loaned the young man his own horse, and then offered both Smith and Hitchcock employment.

Hitchcock, however, soon disappeared with Nordell's horse. Nobody saw or heard anything more from him until some time later, when Smith left Scotsguard for a week. When he returned, he had Nordell's horse. "I asked him where Hitchcock was," Nordell stated to police. "He told me [Hitchcock's] father was sick and had to go to the hospital and he couldn't come."

Though Hitchcock had disappeared, Smith agreed to work for Nordell, and soon enough, he and Harry Bolleson were pitching hay into the livery barn. That's when Smith said, "I'm looking for a buyer for a nice pair of horses that are downstairs."

"So I went in that night and bought the team from him," Bolleson later stated to police.

On October 11, 1915, less than a week after Constable Perry received the original telegram that something was amiss in Scotsguard, Birks arrested Smith at the livery barn.

On October 12, Hitchcock returned to Scotsguard and rode up to Madden's father's homestead. "I'm headin' to Oregon," he said to Madden. "I thought you might like to keep me company." As Madden considered the invitation, Hitchcock confided that police were pursuing both of them regarding some stolen horses.

With that news, Madden took off with Hitchcock, who was riding a bay mare with a white "L" on her face. A chestnut colt, only two months old, was being tagged along. This youngster, probably straight off its mother, had a silver mane and tail, as well as an angry wire cut on its left shoulder.

During their time in the saddle, Madden asked Hitchcock why police had come to be after them. "John Nordell of Scotsguard told me the police had arrested Smith, and were after me," explained Hitchcock. "Smith and I stole horses in the Pendleton area, you know, and now that they're after me, I'm changing my name. D'you think I look like a Charlie Davis?"

As Hitchcock pondered his name change, he and Madden continued riding away from the law. Hitchcock told Madden that he planned to sell his horses in Lethbridge, Alberta, then buy a train ticket and spend the winter in Spokane, Washington. Sometimes a rider's thoughts are never clearer than when he's in the saddle, and the more Madden thought about it, the less he wanted to be on the run. He wanted to go home to his father. Bidding Hitchcock good luck, he turned his horse around and rode back in the direction from which they'd come. Riding on alone, Hitchcock wondered if Madden might turn him in, especially now that he knew his plans. He thought about what he would say to the police if they caught up to him.

Madden wasn't home for long before he was questioned by Birks. He cooperated fully. Later, police were unflattering in their description of Madden: "...not overly gifted with brains, and seems to have a particularly poor memory." But poor memory or not, it was Madden's recollection of all the horse trades that police relied on to follow the thieves' trail.

Smith and Hitchcock were a masterful pair when it came to causing trouble for other people. In fact, once arrested, Smith accused Madden of stealing the goods he himself had been charged with stealing, namely the saddle he'd sold to Robert Stevenson, as well as the horse he'd been riding when he'd been arrested.

But various depositions revealed that it had indeed been Smith, posing as Ted Williams, who had sold the saddle to Robert Stevenson of Scotsguard for $20. Constable Birks brought a Mr. Tubbs all the way from Harlem, Montana, to determine whether or not the saddle — which had the number "44" stamped on its rear and a "4" stamped either side — was his. "The saddle ... I identify positively as the saddle that was stolen from me at Harlem, Montana, by Art Smith last June," said Tubbs. "It is a penitentiary made saddle with peculiar swell and fork. The numbers burnt in the skirts and cantle have been placed there since the saddle was stolen." Tubbs then returned to Montana with his saddle, promising police that he would come back to Canada to appear against Smith at his trial.

But Smith kept his finger pointed squarely at poor Madden. He claimed that it was Madden and Hitchcock who were deeply engaged in horse trading, swapping one stolen horse for another, and that Madden had traded the stolen saddle for Smith's. "Four days below Assiniboia ... Madden changed saddles with me," said Smith. "That is, he traded the Tubbs saddle to me for the saddle I had, as Tubbs' saddle made the back of his horse sore."

Madden admitted he knew the saddle Smith was talking about. He couldn't help but notice when other people had nice things. "It was a round skirted saddle," he recalled, then went on to describe its tall forks, narrow swell, and round bottom stirrups. Smith, attempting to raise the suspicions of police, drew their attention to how well Madden knew the saddle — but was that because he'd stolen it, or because he'd looked at it with envy? "It is the same saddle Art Smith had when he and Perrine Hitchcock caught up to me south of Harlem on June 17," Madden said. His young neck was on the line. How could he prove which of the three men had stolen the saddle?

Madden then made another statement to police. "Smith had this saddle in his possession all the time after we left Harlem, and brought it across the [border] with him. He had it and was using it when I left him and Hitchcock south west of Scotsguard and returned to my home ... I do not think there is another saddle made exactly like it," he said. "The saddle Smith got is a remarkable saddle."

When asked to describe the brands, Madden said, "There is 44 burnt in two places; on the back of the seat and one 4 on each skirt. I do not know who put them there. They were put there on the other side of Assiniboia ... The numbers on the skirt and cantle were burnt there after we crossed the line."

Name That Crook

Authorities questioned Madden's innocence. Could he have stolen the horse and saddle after all? Or was Smith strategically employing the common criminal activity of accusing a naive teenager of his own crime, in hopes the teen would be convicted in his place?

Smith was prepared to elaborate to prove his innocence. "While we were cooking coffee, Madden went up to the CPR fence and cut off two pieces of wire and burned 4s on the Tubbs saddle, and M.S. on the other saddle, and also tried to make a brand, to brand that bay horse."

The accusation sounded plausible, and Smith made it more convincing to the authorities by adding, "A woman was standing in a car used as a living house and watched [Madden] cut the wire. We left there about 9 or 9:30 for Assiniboia. Madden changed saddles with me there."

Madden was beside himself. "I had nothing to do with burning 44 on the saddle. I do not know anything about it. I cut wire. I traded horses once. I had the same saddle right through," he told the justice. "I was hunting for my father's stock. We put up in shacks when we could get them. I never had the saddle of Tubbs unless the one Perrine gave me was his. I had my own saddle when I rode out of Harlem."

"It's a lie!" shouted Smith. "When we got back to Saskatchewan, I went straight to Perrine's place, and helped him shock hay, then I took Nordell's horse back to him, and worked there until I was unfairly arrested for bringing stolen property into Canada."

Stolen Horses

On November 17, 1915, Smith pleaded not guilty to two charges, one of bringing a stolen horse into Canada, the other of bringing a stolen saddle into the country. He elected for a speedy trial, and District Court Judge Smyth remanded him until the Crown prosecutor could fix a trial date.

Madden, meanwhile, was bound over in the sum of $2000 to appear as a witness at the trial. A warrant for Perrine Hitchcock was issued and held at the Shaunavon detachment of the RNWMP.

Smith's trial was held at Gull Lake, Saskatchewan, on December 15, 1915. He appeared before His Honour Judge Smyth. Evidence was the same as that provided at the preliminary hearing with one exception: the defence suggested that Charles Marsh, whose horse had been stolen by Smith after he had given him a ride into Harlem, Montana, had identified the wrong man. However, under cross-examination, Marsh looked at Smith and said, "I know you are the man, for I talked with you for 12 miles…you are the man that rode with me."

Judge Smyth found Art Smith guilty on both charges. Smith's attorney then suggested to the judge that in exchange for a suspended sentence, Smith would be willing to enlist in the army for active service. Judge Smyth acknowledged that while he had allowed prisoners who had been charged with minor offences to do this, he "would not care to risk such a man as the accused, charged with such a serious offence, to mingle with other men of good character." Judge Smyth also noted that this was, "one off the most flagrant cases I have ever had before me." He sentenced Smith to two years in Prince Albert Penitentiary.

Chapter 5
Fanfreluche

Her name was Fanfreluche and she was a national darling, the Canadian Horse of the Year in 1970. Her mother was multiple stakes winner Ciboulette, her father, the great Northern Dancer. Fanfreluche possessed astounding speed, amazing strength, and a competitive mentality. People around the racetrack began to whisper that she might even be able to do the amazing: race against the boys, and win.

Horse races are designed to be fair. Predictable performances are taken into consideration. For instance, young horses are pitted against young horses, and older ones against older ones. But within these predictions of performance is the limitation of sex. Female racehorses seldom have the strength, stamina, and power needed to be serious contenders against stallions.

But Fanfreluche was different. Foaled in 1967, she came in the money an astounding 20 out of 21 racing starts from 1969 to 1970. A consistent stakes winner, she dominated events such as the Benson and Hedges Invitational and the Manitoba Centennial Derby. Her owner, Quebecor Jean-Louis Levesque, was convinced his "Fanny" would bring him what he coveted: the Queen's Plate.

First held in 1860, the Queen's Plate is one of the most prestigious horse races in Canada, and the oldest uninterrupted stakes race in North America. Over the years, many celebrated Thoroughbreds have run "the plate." Winning the race is a major accomplishment, resulting in both wealth and esteem for horse, trainer, and owner.

And in 1971, Fanfreluche had a shot at victory. Though her jockey, Chris Rogers, described the horse as a "chunky little filly," he believed that anyone who could overtake her would win the prestigious race. As one of only two fillies in a field of 15, she ran the two kilometres of the 111th Queen's Plate, finishing an exciting second — an astounding feat in a gruelling horse race of mixed sexes.

One of many outstanding Thoroughbred racehorses bred by Jean-Louis Levesque, Fanfreluche won $238,688 before she was four years old. She became a much sought-after broodmare. In the 1970s, owners of Thoroughbred racing mares dreamed of having their horses bred to the phenomenal Triple Crown stallion, Secretariat. Few mares, however, were deemed good enough to be bred by him. Fanfreluche was one of the exceptions. To Levesque's delight, she was soon in foal to Secretariat.

As a broodmare, Fanfreluche lived in enviable facilities in Paris, Kentucky, where she grazed in warm sunshine and received lavish care. Surprisingly, Levesque did not have her insured, either before or after her joining with Secretariat.

On June 27, 1977, horse racing fans throughout North America were stunned when they glanced at their morning papers. Without prior indication that anything was amiss, front-page headlines screamed the news, "Fanfreluche: Stolen!" She was two months into an 11-month gestation with Secretariat's foal. Reports variously placed her value at between $500,000 and $1.5 million. Levesque, the Kentucky police, and the FBI sat by the phone, waiting for a ransom call. The RCMP was called in on the investigation. Horse racing enthusiasts across the continent held their breath.

Last seen by a watchman in the late afternoon of June 25, Fanfreluche had been grazing with eight other broodmares. When the watchman returned to do a head count that evening, he came up one head short. Assuming a horse was simply out of sight, he didn't look any further. As a result, it was the following morning before workers discovered a fence on the ranch had been tampered with, and that Fanfreluche was missing.

Many people speculated on the motive behind the theft

of the high-profile horse. Would she be bred, and her foals sold for a high price? This seemed unlikely; without a specific demand from the crooks, profits from selling Fanfreluche's foals would be severely limited at best. These foals would be unable to be registered, in which case, as "grade" foals, the youngsters would sell for a small fraction of their true value.

Perhaps Fanfreluche was stolen so that she could be raced under another name. But this, too, seemed doubtful. Regulatory racing agencies are careful about checking a horse's background at the best of times. And after a star horse is stolen, officials scrutinize every piece of paper and every horse that looks even remotely like the missing one. It seemed most likely that Fanfreluche's abductors were simply holding her for ransom. But surprisingly, no one attempted to contact Levesque to collect a ransom or make conditional demands.

As it turned out, the day after Fanfreluche went missing, farmer Harry McPherson came upon the Canadian darling walking along a road more than 240 kilometres from the sight of the theft. Exhausted and afraid, she was in sorry shape, with rope burns around her neck, behind her ears, and around her ankles. McPherson didn't recognize her as anything other than a poor old nag. He took her home, and when nobody came in search of her, he named her "Brandy."

Assuming "Brandy" was a riding horse, McPherson innocently restricted her grazing limits with a solitary strand of electrified wire. He fed her, took care of her, and gave her kindness — something she must have been grateful for after her ordeal.

Months passed. Ever hopeful that Fanfreluche was still alive, Levesque collaborated to post a $25,000 reward for the mare. Reward seekers soon directed investigators to McPherson's farm, where only one week earlier, he had declined a $200 offer for the horse.

Levesque and Fanfreluche were reunited, and less than three months later, she bore a stud colt. Levesque added a dash of magic to the celebrated event. He named the foal *Sain et Sauf,* French for "safe and sound."

The man convicted of Fanfreluche's theft was a horse trainer's grandson by the name of William Michael McCandless, also known as Michael McCandless and William Michael Rhodes. Described as a dreamer and a con artist, McCandless was a known gambler. Like most gamblers, he dreamed of the "big win."

Though details of how and why he was caught and charged with stealing Fanfreluche remain vague, McCandless was convicted of the theft in 1983 and sentenced to four years in jail. But by the 1990s, he was back to shady gambling, and at the age of 51, he was issued a six-count indictment for race fixing.

McCandless knew there were many ways a horse race could be fixed. In 1998, he was charged, in absentia, with engaging in one of the most unscrupulous of these ways: sponging. The process involved sticking a sponge up a horse's nostril and leaving it there. The "sponged" horses all lived in danger of inhaling the sponge beyond the nostril, contracting a serious infection, going into shock, or developing any number of autoimmune diseases as a result of ongoing rejection of the foreign object. They could also have collapsed during a race, causing death or serious injury to all race participants, human and horse. It has been assumed that cutting off a horse's air supply by this means was done in order to hurt the animal's performance and gain a gambling advantage.

The image of a Thoroughbred racehorse thundering round a track, grit flying at his face, nostrils flared and sucking air as he tries to meet the speed he's always had, the sting-sting-sting of the jockey's riding crop as the horse is urged to try harder, giving every last ounce he's got while an uncomfortable sponge presses against the delicate mucous membranes of his nose, blocking his airflow and reducing his oxygen supply, is unnerving. Each day, the sponge becomes increasingly clogged with body fluid, breeding millions of germs, crusting around the edges, and digging further into the animal's sensitive tissue.

McCandless was allegedly stuffing sponges up the nostrils of several horses in Kentucky. Although his intention may not have been to harm the horses, one horse, Class O' Lad, became a mortality statistic. During a race, Class O' Lad's jockey realized the horse was seriously distressed and, mercifully, pulled him up. Upon physical examination, sponges found up Class O' Lad's nostrils were believed to have caused him enough stress to develop laminitis, an agonizing and potentially fatal disease. Just six years old, Class O' Lad was euthanized.

The FBI began an investigation. Because of the potentially lethal result of sponging a horse, a $50,000 reward was offered in hopes that someone would come forward with the information needed to put a quick stop to it. McCandless was fingered for the crime, and though authorities did not know of his whereabouts at the time, he was indicted nevertheless.

Today, McCandless remains at large. Authorities continue to look for him A segment on McCandless was shown on the popular television program *America's Most Wanted*, but failed to produce the necessary information on his whereabouts.

Some people have questioned McCandless's guilt in both crimes, doubting his ability to pull off such feats. McCandless enjoyed a degree of recognition around the racetracks; many people knew him on sight. Some liked him and felt that if he was "sponging," then he must have been forced into it, or perhaps was taking the rap for someone else. His mother also remains convinced of his innocence of both crimes.

And what about Fanfreluche? She produced more foals, 20 in total, and five went on to become stakes winners. In 1999, she died at the impressive age of 32.

Chapter 6
Breeze and Vegas

On March 12, 1993, Delphine Crayford's father-in-law gave her a beautiful gift. He gave her three-year-old Breeze, a grey mare with four black legs, a black mane, and grey freckles on her face. A small horse, Breeze stood just over 15 hands high (five feet tall from the ground to the top of her withers). Due to her uncertain parentage, she was considered a grade horse rather than an identifiable purebred; her sire was believed to be a Quarter Horse, her maternal line was unknown. But while her parentage was uncertain, she was, and remains, an adored gift. "We just seemed to connect right off the bat," says Delphine, her voice gentle with affection. "She was a good little girl, so smart, a real quick learner."

Breeze is the grey on the left, Vegas is on the right

Rather than board Breeze at a riding stable, Delphine kept her right outside the back door, on the family's one-hectare property in Coleman, Alberta. In 1996, Breeze was given a friend in Vegas, a seven-year-old gelding that Delphine and her husband Gary bought for their five-year-old daughter. With a narrow chest and a white star on his forehead, Vegas — like Breeze — had no claim to pedigree blood. But also like Breeze, he quickly won his way into the Crayfords' hearts. "He was an awesome little horse," says Delphine. "He taught my daughter how to ride."

Both horses were regarded as members of the family.

Breeze and Vegas

They were ridden purely for the pleasure of it, and Breeze and Vegas always made it pleasurable. Five years after the horses first came to live on the Crayford property, they were even more loved than they had been in the early days of their arrival.

On June 25, 1998, a family friend drove past the Crayford property. She spotted someone in the front paddock with the horses. At first she thought it was Delphine's husband Gary, but quickly realized the man was too skinny to be him. As she passed the house, she looked over her shoulder to get a second look at the stranger. Unable to identify the man, she felt uneasy — but not uneasy enough to get nosy. Family members were often seen in the paddock with the horses, and lately, they were there more often than usual because Breeze had an infected hind foot that was being treated with penicillin. The neighbour continued to drive on to her own home a short distance away. Meanwhile Gary, a nightshift worker at that time, was upstairs in bed, asleep.

That night, everyone in the Crayford family was in bed by midnight. Delphine's two teenage daughters had both made it home for their 11 o'clock curfew, and when the doors were locked behind the girls, the horses were seen standing beside each other outside.

The following morning, Delphine was the first to get up. Venturing outside in her housecoat, she was surprised not to see the horses. She walked around the property and soon noticed that the back gate of the pasture was open. With mounting anxiety, Delphine ran through the open gate, then up the hill and across the pipeline, where she saw that the main gate was also open. Stunned, she rushed back to the house, phoned the police, and dressed quickly, alerting the rest of the family to her discovery as she did so.

Officers from two police departments — the RCMP and Crowsnest Pass Police —arrived at the Crayford house shortly after Delphine's call. Their investigations did not inspire confidence from the Crayfords. "The RCMP thought the horses were just 'out'," says Delphine. "They kept saying 'Oh, don't worry about it. They'll turn up'." But Delphine knew differently. "My horses are happy, and they don't open gates," she told one police officer.

Despite the lacklustre investigation, one officer did think it necessary to do a check of the rural pastures and try to get more information. However, when Delphine asked for the wide band at the top of her pasture gate to be finger-printed, police refused. The Crayfords sensed that authorities didn't think this was the theft of something valuable. "The minute it's an animal it's 'big deal'," says Delphine. Though one police officer found a witness in the area who claimed to have seen the horses being led up the road, the witness later recanted her statement. No reason was given for her contradiction, and authorities didn't press the matter for an explanation.

After the police left the Crayford house, the family, distraught and frustrated, walked together to the back of the property. As tears streamed down their faces, their shock and sense of loss was almost more than they could bear. Then they saw hoofprints on the ground.

"We found the tracks," recalls Delphine. "We followed them to a subdivision. We knew it was them because one horse was just putting the toe of the foot down." That track belonged to Delphine's beloved Breeze. Even with the pain of her infected foot, Breeze was gentle and kind, trying to keep her weight off her sore heel while walking obediently for her abductor. How the villain must have appreciated her sweet natured cooperativeness. A sudden burst of hope propelled the family forward as they followed the tracks. But their hearts quickly sunk when the hoofprints came to an abrupt end, and trailer marks took over. "They were loaded into a trailer…and then they were gone," says Delphine.

The next morning, the Crayfords rose early to begin another day of searching. Knowing it is not uncommon for stolen horses to be taken to slaughterhouses, Delphine and her family made their way to the nearest one, located an hour away in Fort MacLeod, Alberta. The slaughterhouse had a little holding pen where a person could drop a horse off after hours, putting the necessary paperwork through a slot in the door and leaving the horse in the pen. But Breeze and Vegas weren't there, and the Crayfords left the slaughterhouse to continue their pursuit.

Family friends came out to help with the search. A poster was quickly put together and taken to a local print shop, where 500 colour copies were printed. Website notices were posted, and a reward was offered for the return of the missing animals. The family also contacted the local media, phoned brand inspectors, and visited as many auction marts as they could. At a few of the auction marts, Delphine heard rumours that some brand inspectors would allow horses to go through the auction without proof of ownership. "I don't know if that was true," she says. Although sellers are supposed to prove ownership, a fake bill of sale would enable a thief to sell an animal that's not his or hers to sell.

About a week after Breeze and Vegas were stolen, a local radio station ran a feature on the horses and interviewed Delphine. Three weeks later, Delphine appeared on a morning television talk show, and soon after, a local news crew came out and filmed the area around the Crayford house for a segment on the thefts.

Then the leads started to come in. "Some leads were for ridiculous places," says Delphine, "but you have to check them all out. One lead turned out not to be even the right colour of horses!"

A livestock investigator in Calgary phoned Delphine after hearing her talk on the radio. Located mostly in Canada's western provinces, livestock investigators are government agents or law enforcement officers who check manifests for the proper number and description of animals, determine that brands do in fact belong to the person claiming ownership, and investigate missing livestock. The livestock investigator in Calgary suggested a few resources for Delphine, and put her in touch with a local police officer who was considered knowledgeable about rural affairs. The investigator then contacted a U.S. brand inspector (in case the thieves tried to take the horses across the border), and told Delphine that he believed the horses might have been seized by an organized crime element operating on a circuitous route from Calgary to Montana.

After the investigator's phone calls, the groundwork of the search had to be done by Delphine and her family. And sadly, even once this groundwork was done, the whereabouts of Breeze and Vegas were still unknown.

As the Crayfords continued to search for clues, Delphine's sister began to wonder if rodeo participants might have been involved. She had put some reining work into Breeze because Delphine was going to learn to rein. During the training time, Delphine's sister had used Breeze as an entry horse at the opening of a couple of rodeos. Had someone at the rodeo seen how adorable Breeze was, watched how easily she loaded into the trailer, and decided to steal her?

Of course, the thief could have been someone entirely outside of the rodeo, someone who was brazen enough to check the horses in their own pasture to see how approachable they were and how easy they would be to catch. Someone sinister and shameless enough to do this while Gary was asleep at only an arm's length away.

Three months after the horses disappeared, Delphine

began to consider contacting an animal communicator to help in the search. Delphine knew these specialists were contracted to perform a variety of services, most of which centred on communicating telepathically with an animal. She also knew that horse owners sometimes turned to animal communicators if their veterinarians were unable to identify a horse's specific ailment, and she had heard the testimonials claiming the communicators were often able to identify the condition. Some animal communicators say they are able to converse with animals regardless of whether the animas are dead or alive. Others claim only to speak with the living. And most claim that they can receive information from the animal while on the phone with the animal's owner.

Delphine had seen an animal communicator promoted on television, and the message suggested that this woman's services were affordable. For months, Delphine debated whether to contact her. Almost a year after the horses disappeared, she bit the bullet and phoned the animal communicator. But the cost proved to be much more than Delphine had expected. She was told that for $500 U.S. she could have half an hour on the phone with her. However, for a much smaller fee, she could ask two quick questions. Perhaps answers to two questions would be better than nothing.

Delphine agonized over how to phrase her two questions in order to get as much information as she could. Finally, she asked: "Do you know who took them?" The communicator answered that "Alice and Raymond" were responsible for taking Breeze and Vegas. Wondering how two first names would get her any closer to her horses, Delphine then asked, "Do you know where they are?" The communicator answered that the horses were in Butte, Montana.

Delphine hadn't thought it possible for the horses to be taken across the border. But, armed with the vague information the animal communicator had offered, she loaded her car up with posters, and the family headed off to Butte early on a Sunday morning. "It's an eight hour drive, and we had to be back that day," says Delphine, "so we didn't have much time to spend."

The family was able to visit with a brand inspector in Butte, but the visit did not bring much comfort. To their amazement, they learned it was actually easy to get a horse into the United States. With the border only two hours from the Crayford home, there were suddenly many new possibilities for Breeze and Vegas's whereabouts — new possibilities, but no new leads.

Only months after the family's visit to Butte, Delphine's suspicion that nobody appreciated the value of what had been stolen was reinforced. "I got a phone call from a female police officer," she explains. "She was retiring and wanted to tie up some loose ends, so she was closing the case. I told her that the case wasn't closed, the horses hadn't been found, but she insisted she wanted to tie up the loose ends."

Of course, tying up loose ends is something Delphine has been unable to do. "Not knowing means you have no closure…you don't get over it, " she says, her voice cracking. She still gets choked up when she drives past a grey horse in a field, wondering if it could be Breeze. "I've no idea what happened to the two of them. Maybe if the right person was to hear about the theft and be honest … maybe someday I'll be able to say, 'I got my horses back.' I'm still looking."

Chapter 7
Khalett

Horse thieves do not limit themselves to stealing from pastures, barns, or stables to get their prizes. Most are perpetually alert for any opportunity they can exploit. Such an opportunity presented itself on Vancouver Island in the summer of 1997, when Darlene Gordon and her beloved horse Khalett went for a trail ride along a secluded logging road.

A beautiful Arabian mare, Khalett was born in 1983 on Darlene's 15 hectares in Courtenay, British Columbia. Darlene, who was present at the birth, combined the names of the foal's dam and sire; the Texan sire was River Song Khalid and the dam, Daodar Marett. Khalett's "bay" colouring meant that she was one of various shades of chestnut, accented with a black mane, muzzle, tail, and stockings.

As Khalett matured, Darlene decided to use her as a trail-riding horse, and she rode the mare in an old, unusual Toptani jumping saddle. Because her property was small, Darlene was always on the lookout for new places to ride. She didn't want Khalett to become bored with riding on the same paths all the time. The two travelled many new and interesting trails together. "She was a very good trail horse," remembers Darlene with obvious affection.

Accustomed to years of trail riding, Khalett had grown into a steady, dependable horse, always taking Darlene safely through new terrain, and enjoying the outings. In 1997, Khalett was 14 years old. The pair had been trail riding together for about a dozen years, and they were always happy to find new terrain and fresh trails to explore. On July 29, 1997, at about 6:00 p.m., Darlene loaded Khalett into her two-horse bumper pull trailer, and then drove to a new trail that she'd found about eight kilometres from home.

It was a beautiful sunny evening, and by 6:30 p.m., the two had started their ride on an old logging road surrounded by dense bush. The unfamiliar area resembled a tropical forest. "The growth was so dense that a person would have a hard time walking through it, let alone a horse," recalls Darlene. After riding for about an hour and a half, the pair came around a bend to find themselves facing — of all things — a flock of 30 emus! Making peculiar noises, the large birds

Khalett

Khalett

began to approach Khalett and Darlene, causing Khalett to become fearful and restless. Darlene dismounted to try to scare off the birds and calm her horse. "If I'd have been smart, I'd have taken her away right away," says Darlene. Instead, as she tried to reassure the horse, Khalett suddenly bolted. Darlene lost her grip on the reins, and the horse ran back from whence she'd come. "I never saw her again," says Darlene.

Darlene followed Khalett by keeping an eye on the horse's hoofprints on the trail. She noted that for a short time, Khalett had run at a full gallop, then slowed down and eventually walked in the direction of Darlene's horse trailer. Hoping that Khalett might be waiting for her at the trailer, Darlene's concerns escalated when the hoofprints stopped at a water-filled ditch. Convinced that Khalett would not have jumped the ditch, Darlene began to wander around the unfamiliar area in search of her mare.

With no sign of the horse, Darlene returned to the logging road where she'd last seen the hoofprints. The road was lined with a few semi-isolated homes, and a handful of residents were milling around. Darlene asked if anyone had seen a riderless horse. "No one had seen her," recalls Darlene. "It's not as if they could have missed her. She was all saddled up, and her reins would've been flying."

Darlene was at a loss over where Khalett could have gone. The density of growth off the logging road was ideal for a cougar or small animal to hide in, but not for a horse to go through. "When a horse gets lost it's usually on a road, and they're found very quickly because there's no place for them to go," explains Darlene. "The bush is just too dense for them to go into."

When Darlene chose to head off and search in a certain direction, a couple of people standing along the road finally spoke up, saying that they'd seen the horse and that she'd gone a different way. Darlene went where they directed her, only to have other people along the road say the horse had taken another route. "You're running around looking for a horse and you know damned well that people are lying to you because she didn't vanish into thin air."

Darlene grew increasingly frustrated and panicked. She was running around in circles, and the residents on the trails were controlling the direction in which she travelled. "I think these people kept trying to get me to go in the opposite direction. They were not nice people," she says. "But how many times do you expect people to steal your horse? It's inconceivable to me, but obviously they must have known where she was. If I'd been where there were no people around, I think I'd have gone where I thought she was, and found her."

Khalett's hoofprints at the water-filled ditch suggested that she'd milled around that one spot for probably several minutes. Darlene wondered if someone had come up to Khalett, taken the lead rope, and led her away. "There could only have been about 15 minutes between the time she got to that spot and the time that I did," she explains. "She had to have been just led off to the bush and held there, watching me while I was worried that she'd carried on and would get into traffic. [The thieves] were opportunists because [they] could see me running around, frantic."

At one point, two young men who were hanging around asked Darlene if there was a reward for finding the horse. But she hadn't even reached that stage of thought. "I did think it was a bit strange to ask about a reward for a horse that was supposedly just down the road a bit," she says. "When I look back, I should've said 'yes' and I wonder if I'd said that if it would've made a difference."

Stolen Horses

By 11 o'clock that night, Darlene was exhausted; she drove home with her empty horse trailer. In total disbelief, she grew more and more certain that Khalett had been stolen, and that the thieves were keeping her out of sight from searching eyes. "I was hoping I was wrong, but why couldn't I find her?" she still asks. "It was really upsetting and terrible. They used to *hang* people for this!"

As she drove onto her property, her spirits sunk even more. "I was exhausted," she remembers, her voice breaking. "I had been walking around and was really strung out, and the other horses came running over, whinnying to welcome [Khalett] home, and she wasn't there."

Darlene fed her dogs then tried to sleep. Up at 4:30 the next morning, she phoned some friends who came to help her look for the horse. She phoned auction houses and people who trailer horses from one location to another. One generous man hired a helicopter to go up and look for Khalett. Another friend brought his own dependable trail horse along to search the trials and possibly draw Khalett out of the bush in the event that she was hiding. However, when this horse refused to cross the water-filled ditch, Darlene became even more certain that Khalett hadn't gone over it either. She distributed flyers, and on them, indicated that a reward was being offered. The amount wasn't stipulated. A few days later, a friend contacted the RCMP on Darlene's behalf. "He said the police were really reluctant to bother," she remembers. "I think it might have been a little different if she'd been stolen out of the field." However reluctantly, police did open a file on the horse.

Soon after Khalett's disappearance, rumours about a dead horse in the area began to circulate. But no one ever contacted Darlene personally about such a find. The stories always came third or fourth-hand from hunters or surveyors. Worse, residents along the logging road kept insisting that Khalett was nowhere to be found. "I think they knew who had her but didn't want to say anything," says Darlene. Sometimes she would bump into people who knew her horse was missing, and they would say: "Oh, I heard you found your mare dead." But none of these people ever actually enquired about the source of this news. "It would have been better if I had found her dead," Darlene says. "At least I'd have known where she was."

By early August of 1997, Darlene realized her horse could be anywhere. She knew that British Columbia auction houses did not require proof of ownership to sell a horse; Khalett could have passed through an auction house as an unregistered — but flashy — Arabian, and no one would have raised an eyebrow. Added to this setback was the fact that Darlene lived on Vancouver Island. The horse could easily have been loaded into a horse trailer, driven onto the ferry, and ended up on the mainland to be sold there without question.

For the next month, Darlene kept looking, receiving countless false leads along the way. She received phone calls from people saying they'd seen the horse weeks before, but didn't know where the animal was now; and from people saying they'd seen the horse in the southern U.S., or Montreal, or any other assortment of places. One call from British Columbia's interior sounded promising. The people who made the call subsequently convinced the RCMP to investigate. "A female officer went up but didn't see the horse," says Darlene. Oddly, during the conversation with police, the suspects implied that they knew Darlene well, and that they had purchased a buckskin mare from her. But Darlene has never owned — or sold — a buckskin horse.

Hoping to draw the necessary information that would allow her to find her horse, Darlene put up a web page and posted a $1000 reward. Lots of people visited the website, and for a long time, Darlene opened up the abundant e-mails generated by the visits, eager to find a diamond lead. "Mostly it was just idiots making stupid statements, or else it was kindly folks who were sympathetic, but unfortunately couldn't help," says Darlene. People e-mailed her from as far away as California, often telling stories that only served to etch her wounds deeper.

Darlene realized that with the passage of time, it was becoming less likely that Khalett would be returned; the longer the horse was missing, the harder it would be for someone to return the animal without admitting some complicity in her disappearance. Darlene decided to make the risk worth it. She upped the reward to $10,000. "I would have

Khalett

had a bit of trouble coming up with that amount, but thought it would be worth it if it brought a chance of recovering her, or at least knowing where she was."

And, even though she didn't believe in the power of psychics, Darlene called one. "The reading was so vague it was impossible to follow. Some cowboy had her on the coast. It was useless, but I had to try," she says. Friends who also believed they possessed psychic abilities told her that Khalett was in a specific field, but when they went to the spot, the horse wasn't there. "I would get this hope up, and then it would be dashed. It was like getting kicked in the face again."

One small consolation was received much later. Darlene drove through Fort McLeod and stopped off at the slaughterhouse. Even though no one could help her, Khalett's picture was still posted in the office with her information, including a notation about a fungal infection that had been evident on the animal's lower legs — not a serious infection, more of a nuisance thing. Darlene hoped that if Khalett had found her way to caring people, that they might get a veterinarian to look at the infection, and the vet might ultimately help return her to her rightful owner.

Eventually, after newspaper, magazine, radio, and television coverage of Khalett's disappearance failed to turn up the horse, and after having spent several hundred dollars in advertising and posters, Darlene concluded that she was unlikely to ever see Khalett again. She never believed such a nightmare could happen. "It made me a little disgusted with some people, and a lot less trusting than I used to be," she says. "It's so upsetting. I was lied to, to my face. But I still think about Khalett and wonder what happened to her, or if she's even still alive."

An avid and frequent rider before Khalett's disappearance, Darlene has not ridden the trails since she lost her horse. Despite how much she used to love horses and riding, she has now given up everything that has to do with them. "Better to sell the horses and know what happened to them, than this," she explains sadly. She has sold her horse trailer and all but one of her remaining horses, a Morab gelding who reminds Darlene of Khalett. His sale will be completed soon.

Six years after Khalett's disappearance, Darlene still thinks about her and wonders what fate awaited the animal. "I still involuntarily look for her when I go past a field of horses," she says. "It has been an upsetting few years. Not knowing is the worst."

And the nightmare of not knowing has been compounded by the fact that Darlene believes there are people out there who do know what happened to her mare. "The other bad thing is knowing that someone knows but has deliberately not told me," she says. "Some evil person who doesn't know me, and I have no idea why they'd want to be so hurtful."

Chapter 8
Mekeezun

I n the late summer of 2000, an American Paint Horse named Mekeezun was nibbling Alberta grass when she was purchased by Christine Pohlkamp of Guelph, Ontario. Christine had gone though the usual long-distance purchase procedure, making phone calls, seeing videotapes of the horse in action, but never actually meeting the animal. The fact that seven-year-old Mekeezun was in foal with her first baby was a mixed blessing. Christine wasn't a breeder. She just wanted a nice, flashy horse to ride.

And Mekeezun was flashy. When she arrived in Guelph by horse trailer, she was heavy in foal, but Christine fell in love with her on sight. Mekeezun's unique black and white markings on her left shoulder looked very much like an inverted map of Italy, a feature that led to her name, which is Ojibway for "the boot." She also sported a nifty little brand, low on her right flank, which looked like the roof of a house overtop a circle.

Soon after her arrival, Mekeezun dropped her foal on the ground. Christine witnessed the birth, a process that touched her deeply on both an emotional and spiritual level. Thinking that her work was over, Mekeezun demonstrated her gentle disposition not by standing protectively over her foal, but by being warm and sociable to anyone who came around to see the new baby. Mekeezun's large, round brown eyes endeared her to everyone who showed up.

Despite Christine's original intention to have a riding horse, it wasn't long before Mekeezun was in foal again. She carried the growing life for the mandatory 11 months or so, then, once again, dropped the foal in front of Christine and went off to hang around with nearby humans.

Soon after the second birth, Christine felt the urge to own a Friesian horse. She knew that Friesians were expensive. When her finances wouldn't stretch far enough for the horse she wanted, Christine decided to breed Mekeezun to a Friesian stallion. This was to be the mare's last foal before becoming a full-time riding horse.

With her two previous foals, Mekeezun's sides had expanded as the fetuses grew. But with the half-Friesian fetus, her sides didn't expand much. Instead, her belly kept getting closer to the ground, making her look more sway-backed than pregnant. But Mekeezun didn't appear laboured with the fetal position, and carried on as usual.

Christine was eager for the birth of this foal, an event due to take place at the end of March 2003. A few weeks before each of Mekeezun's prior deliveries, Christine had taken the mare from her home to a foaling stable about 15 kilometres away. Due to the delicate disposition of horses, pregnant mares need to be monitored carefully when they go into labour. Foaling stables provide extra roomy stalls, as well as specialized food and careful monitoring, prior to and following the delivery. Attendants watch the mares for signs of impending labour, and once these signs are observed, the mare is taken to her stall. There she is monitored 24 hours a day by way of cameras discretely hooked up inside the stall. The cameras avoid disturbing the mare in her early stages of labour while relaying a clear picture of the horse and the progression of the labour to the attendants.

Christine liked the foaling stable that Mekeezun had been to for the previous pregnancies. She liked the caring, watchful attendants, and she was happy with the way Mekeezun and her foals had been tended. So, not surprisingly, she opted to bring the mare to the same place a couple of months before she was due to drop the Friesian cross.

During her times of "confinement," Mekeezun had befriended another broodmare, Spot, who delivered her foals around the same time as Mekeezun. The two pastured together, and in the barn, were stalled directly across from each other. The stalls were large enough to house a full-grown horse and her rapidly growing youngster. The front wall of each stall had a dual purpose. On the inside, the wall served to enclose the front of the stall, providing safety, privacy, and shelter from drafts coming through the barn on windy days. On the outside, it was the barrier of the aisle that stretched through the length of the barn. A steel gate across the entrance to the stall prevented the horse or foal from getting out; once closed, the heavy, hinged gate locked securely with a dowel-shaped lock.

As she had before, Mekeezun settled in quickly at the foaling stable, perhaps because once again, Spot was there, too. Two or three times a week, during the coldest days of winter, Christine drove to the stable to groom and exercise the mare. She attached a lead shank to MeKeezun's halter, and the two of them walked outside in the nippy air, their feet crunching the snow in a two-step, four-step rhythm, and their breath making puffy white clouds as they exhaled. During these exercise sessions, Christine talked to Mekeezun, telling her stories about what the animals at home were doing, and of course, how much she was looking forward to the arrival of the foal.

Sometimes, when Christine brushed the mare, she gently laid her head against the horse's belly, hoping to hear or feel some indication that the foal was alive and well. And as she gave, so she received: once, as she listened for the baby, she was kicked squarely in the head by the foal!

Less than a week before Meekezun was due to foal, Christine had to go to Halifax, Nova Scotia, on business. She visited the mare before she left. "It was Wednesday, and it was really cold. I told her, 'don't have your baby while I'm gone! I'll be back two days before you're due to foal. Wait for me!'" With that, Christine left for the East Coast.

The evening of Saturday, March 22, was cold and dark. At 7:00 p.m., the stable owner brought Mekeezun into the barn and locked her in her stall for the night. Mekeezun looked across the aisle at Spot while the owner put grain in their buckets. Then each horse buried her head in her respective pail and chewed rhythmically. As the two mares ate their grain, they periodically leaned over to look across the aisle at each other.

The stable owner inspected each of the horses. Mekeezun's udders were "waxing up," a sure sign that foaling would take place within the next three or four days. The drama of birth was starting to unfold, but a bigger drama was about to begin.

One hour later, the owner made a safety check. When she entered the barn, she knew immediately that something was wrong. The gate to Mekeezun's stall was on the floor. The stall was empty. The woman frantically searched through the barn, but to no avail.

Because Christine was out of town, her partner, Grant Robertson, and a mutual friend were called. With a slew of other people, they searched for the horses on foot and by ATV until 2:00 a.m., combing the back roads and trudging through frozen swamp. Later that morning, a number of Christine and Grant's friends went looking on horseback, paying special attention to farms that were home to other horses in case the mare had uncharacteristically gone "visiting."

The following day, the Ontario Provincial Police were called in. As everyone searched, someone found hoofprints, wide and shoeless, in the dirt on the road near the foaling stable. The hoofprints circled the tire tracks of a truck and trailer.

Christine was oblivious to the ongoing panic and potential danger her horse was in. When Grant picked her up from the airport the next day, he said, "I've got something to tell you. We have to talk." When they arrived home, Grant sat her on the side of the bed and gently told her, "Mekeezun is missing."

Christine promptly went into shock. "My heart just stopped," she says. Her mind racing, she wondered if the mare could have given birth standing, tied up in a trailer. The very thought gave her chills. "It felt like … a personal attack. It was so traumatic and awful. People have no idea," she says.

While the search for Mekeezun continued, police asked Christine if she could think of anybody who might have had something against her. But neither she nor Grant could think of anyone. Christine's frustration mounted when one of the officers informed her that they couldn't broadcast

Mekeezun's brand or markings on the police computer system. "He said, 'If she had a tattoo we'd send out the number,' but because she doesn't have a tattoo, he wouldn't," Christine recalls, shaking her head. "I told him that her brand is easy to describe, just like a child's clothing, and he said, 'It's not a child'."

While Mekeezun's whereabouts remained unknown, everyone tried to fit the pieces of the puzzle together. It was hard to imagine how the horse could have lifted the heavy steel gate off its hinges. For safety reasons, there were no ledges or gaps that the horse could have used for leverage. The stall bore no evidence of struggle that might suggest another animal had come into the barn and frightened the mare.

Could Mekeezun have simply gone off somewhere to have her foal alone? With a history of quiet foaling, there was no reason to believe she would have taken such drastic measures to do this. Besides, her grain was still in the feed bucket, and a pregnant mare, in all likelihood, would devour that grain unless a serious force — like a human — had taken her away from it. Then there were those tire marks and hoofprints to consider. And so, Christine found herself with an unsettling mystery and a huge hole in her life.

On Tuesday, March 25, Christine was giving a business-related workshop when she received three messages on her cellular telephone, all in quick succession. The first message was from her veterinarian's wife. The message said, "We've found your mare and foal, and the foal's in distress."

Anxiously, Christine listened to the second message: "We've found your mare and the baby's okay." The third message said: "We found your mare and foal, and since we can't reach you, we've called the owner of the foaling barn, who's coming out to get them."

Within half an hour Mekeezun and her little filly foal were loaded into a trailer and driven back to the foaling barn. Christine's veterinarian inspected both animals and performed a postnatal examination. He estimated that the foal had been born the previous day. Once again Christine was thrown into an emotional upheaval. Where and how was Mekeezun found?

As it turned out, she was discovered two concessions and three kilometres away from the foaling farm. A woman who worked at a training stable had gone out to bring in their horses when she spotted Mekeezun with her foal in the field. She knew instantly the mare didn't belong on the property. "This property had been searched several times for Mekeezun," explains Christine. "A flyer that had been posted on the bulletin board of the barn instructed where to call in the event the horse was found."

Though relieved that Mekeezun and the foal were safe, Christine couldn't help feeling some regret as well. "I missed out on the birth," she says. "I was present for all of the pregnancy and every vet test, and I didn't get to see the baby being born. It still makes me mad that [the thief] took that away from me."

Mekeezun

She is also plagued by unanswered questions. "I sometimes wonder if whoever took her didn't realize that she was pregnant until after they took her. She was completely clean when she was found. There was no mud, or leaves, or anything on either her or the foal, which leads [me] to believe that she foaled in a barn."

Of course, it's possible that whoever took Mekeezun didn't realize until after the fact that she'd be difficult to unload. The horse's distinctive markings were easily recognizable, and her small brand would not have gone unnoticed at an auction sale. Without proper documentation, proving ownership of the horse could have been difficult.

And how would a thief have explained the foal? It's possible that whoever picked Mekeezun up hadn't known she was in foal, or if they had, hoped to find a purebred Paint foal on the ground instead of a strange looking crossbred foal of a solid colour. Perhaps the thief or thieves just got scared, and decided to leave the horse somewhere in hopes that people would think she'd somehow been overlooked during the search.

Whatever the case, as soon as Mekeezun was found, police closed the investigation. "I asked them to continue looking for the thief, but they refused," says Christine, shaking her head in disbelief.

A local newspaper reported that Mekeezun had been found and was safely home. But was she unscarred? Historically, Mekeezun had always been willing to share her babies with other horses and humans. "When she first came back, she was a bit skittish," says Christine. "She wasn't as social. She was reluctant to be touched or even brushed, and would walk away. It took about a month and a half for this to settle. She wasn't like this with either of her other foals. I would say this traumatized her."

If horses could talk, Christine would know for sure how the horsenapping affected Mekeezun. Horses do have mental flashbacks; unpleasant experiences are readily recalled by a sight, sound, or smell they associate with a bad time. But until more information about the theft can be found, no one knows whether the mare was treated well or poorly. Mekeezun is quietly holding on to the information that only she and her abductors know.

"It still bothers me," says Christine, gulping hard. "Just talking about it bothers me. I wish I knew who did it because I've got a big issue with him ... I still get nightmares."

Bibliographic Note

John McEvoy has additional details about the Fanfreluche theft in his book, *Great Horse Racing Mysteries*, published by The Blood-Horse Inc., Lexington, Kentucky.

Acknowledgments

My sincere thanks to those people who endured the hardship of recalling their arduous experiences with horse theft so that this book could be written: Delphine Crayford, Darlene Gordon, and Christine Pohlkamp.

Thanks to the RCMP, and to Ontario Premier Ernie Eves's staff for considering my deadline. Thanks also to The National Archives of Canada, and the *Toronto Star*. All quotes found in the first four chapters of this book were taken directly from historical police reports, and those in the Fanfreluche chapter were taken from the *Toronto Star* archives.

Finally, thanks to the following people: Rossie historian Sandra Wyman, for her colourful details and added extras; Sandra Phinney, for her support and friendship, which I cherish; Dan Streeter, for his willingness to teach me how to do better, his patience and friendship. You're the best! And lastly, to Kara Turner and Jill Foran, for trusting me to deliver.

About the Author

Dorothy Pedersen has worked in various facets of the horse industry for over 20 years. An award-winning writer and public speaker, she holds an honours diploma in equine studies, as well as a certificate of horsemanship.

After having her own horses stolen in 1992, Dorothy undertook extensive research into the crime of horse theft, and has continued to investigate this aspect of crime — including its prevention and detection — ever since. She has had articles on horse and livestock theft published throughout North America for 15 years, and has been told by two government sources that she probably knows more about this crime than anyone else in the country. In 1996, she was asked to consult with the Ontario Provincial Police, and provided the information that led to the creation of their livestock database.

She is currently drafting her next writing project, a handbook on livestock theft prevention and detection. Dorothy lives in Grand Valley, Ontario, and owns a fully retired horse.

Photo Credits

Cover: Dorothy Pedersen; **Darlene Gordon:** page 83; **Delphine Crayford:** page 72.

AMAZING STORIES™

RIDING ON THE WILD SIDE

Tales of Adventure in the Canadian West

HUMAN INTEREST/BACKCOUNTRY
by Dale Portman

RIDING ON THE WILD SIDE
Tales of Adventure in the Canadian West

*"Suddenly, there was a crashing noise to our left
and out of the timber came about 20 head of
horses and a few bewildered elk followed
by a couple of yelling cowboys."*

This fascinating collection of stories is about
working horses and the people who make a
living riding them in Canada's mountain
national parks. Imagine chasing a herd of wild
horses, galloping at full speed toward an
impenetrable forest ... and you get a sense of the
excitement of the backcountry life.

 True stories. Truly Canadian.

ISBN 1-55153-985-3

AMAZING STORIES™

LEGENDARY SHOW JUMPERS

The Incredible Stories of
Great Canadian Horses

ANIMAL/SPORT
by Debbie Gamble-Arsenault

LEGENDARY SHOW JUMPERS
The Incredible Stories of Great Canadian Horses

"He could be so gentle and quiet, but when he got in the ring he got so excited we couldn't hold him. …But I wasn't afraid of him."
Louis Welsh on Barra Lad

Once in a while a horse comes along that is extraordinary. Air Pilot, Barra Lad, and Big Ben have all had their turn at being the brightest star blazing in the show-jumping sky. For more than 100 years, great Canadian high-flying horses have provided spectators with exhilarating displays of their jaw-dropping talent and love of jumping.

 True stories. Truly Canadian.

ISBN 1-55153-980-2

OTHER AMAZING STORIES

These titles are available wherever you buy books. If you have trouble finding the book you want, call the Altitude order desk at 1-800-957-6888, e-mail your request to: orderdesk@altitudepublishing.com or visit our Web site at www.amazingstories.ca

New AMAZING STORIES titles are published every month. If you would like more information, e-mail your name and mailing address to: amazingstories@altitudepublishing.com.

THE HEART OF A HORSE
Poignant Tales and Humorous Escapades

"With the first jump, I would be trying to bring that old pony's head up and around to stop him. By the second jump, I was already looking for the perfect place to land. By the third jump I had mentally said my 'Goodbye Cruel World' speech. By the fourth I was picking dirt out from between my teeth."

This collection of heart-warming tales of one woman's passion for horses covers the spectrum from breeding and training, to adventures involving grizzly bears, uncooperative cows, and a truck named Herman. Gayle Bunney's comic insights bring to life the wild and wonderful experience of living with horses.

 True stories. Truly Canadian.

ISBN 1-55153-994-2